ollege

AUTOBIOGRAPHIX

WITHDRAWN

DARK HORSE BOOKS™

TABLE OF CONTENTS

Cover art by Will Eisner

Cover design by Paul Hornschemeier

DIANA SCHUTZ
Editor

PAUL HORNSCHEMEIER
Designer

CHRIS HORN
Digital Production

MIKE RICHARDSON
Publisher

AUTOBIOGRAPHIX

Published by
Dark Horse Books
A division of Dark Horse Comics, Inc.
10956 SE Main Street
Milwaukie, Oregon 97222

First edition: December 2003
ISBN 1-59307-038-1

1 3 5 7 9 10 8 6 4 2
Printed in Canada

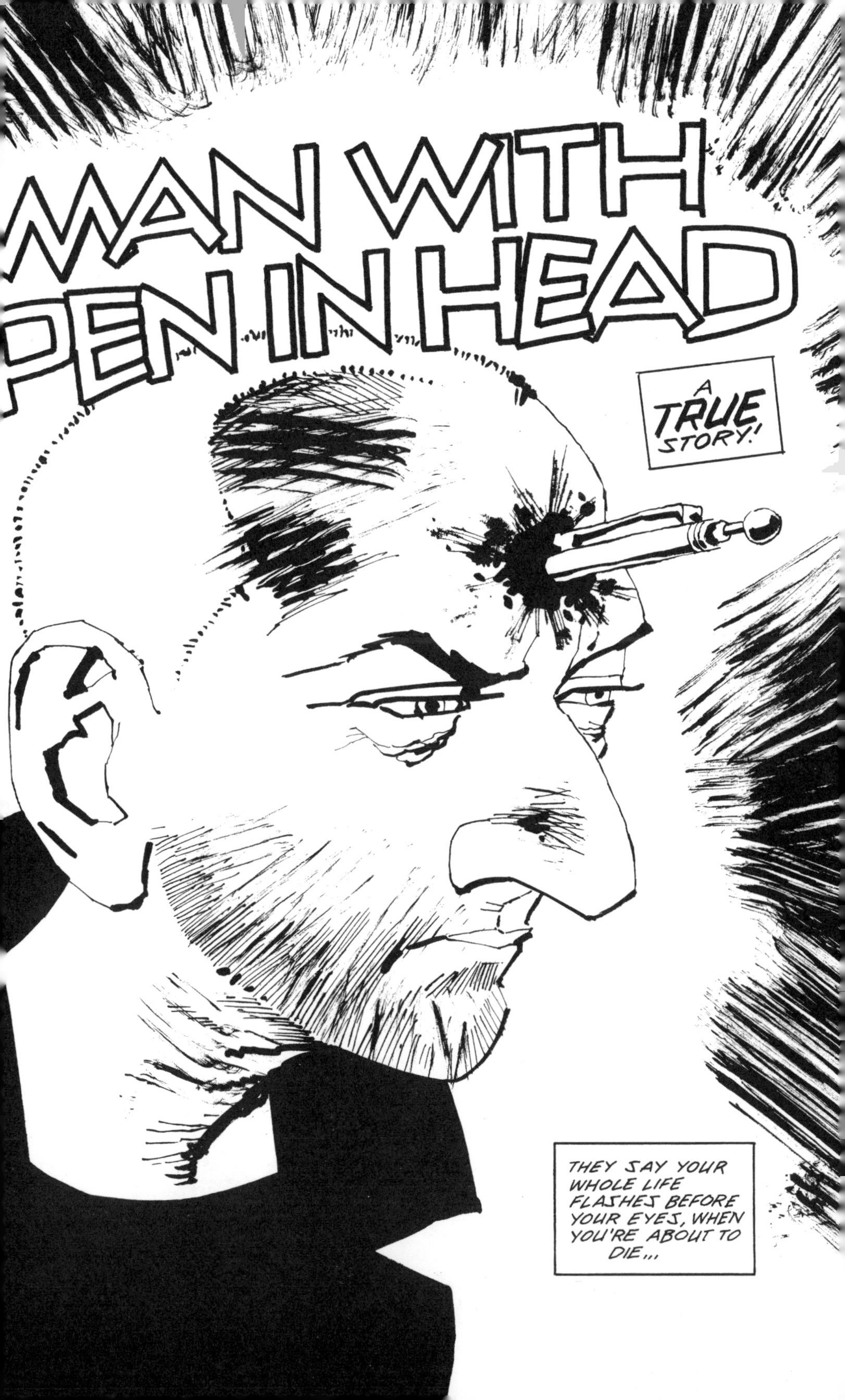
MAN WITH PEN IN HEAD
A TRUE STORY!
THEY SAY YOUR WHOLE LIFE FLASHES BEFORE YOUR EYES, WHEN YOU'RE ABOUT TO DIE...

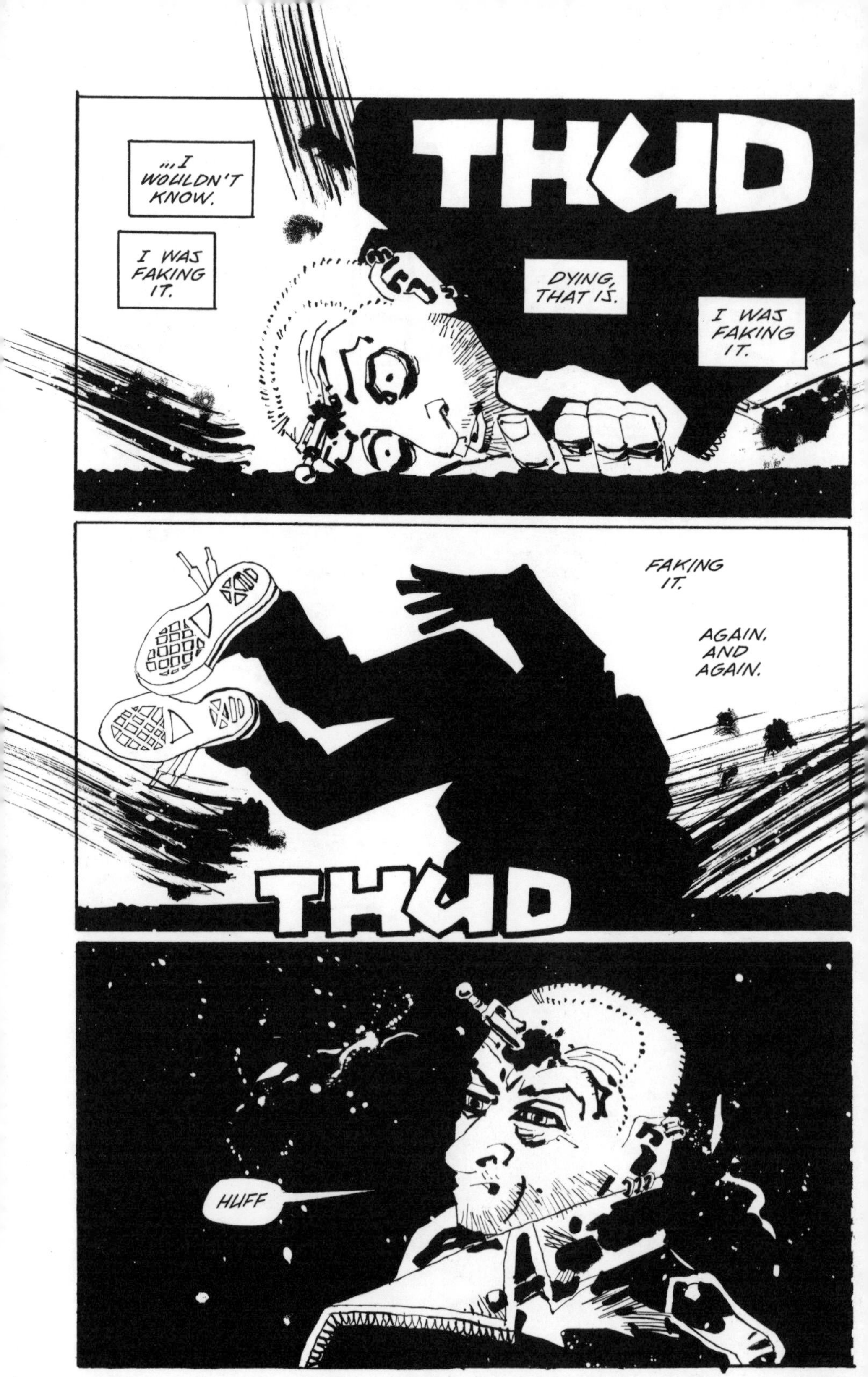

...I WOULDN'T KNOW.
I WAS FAKING IT.
THUD
DYING, THAT IS.
I WAS FAKING IT.
FAKING IT.
AGAIN. AND AGAIN.
THUD
HUFF

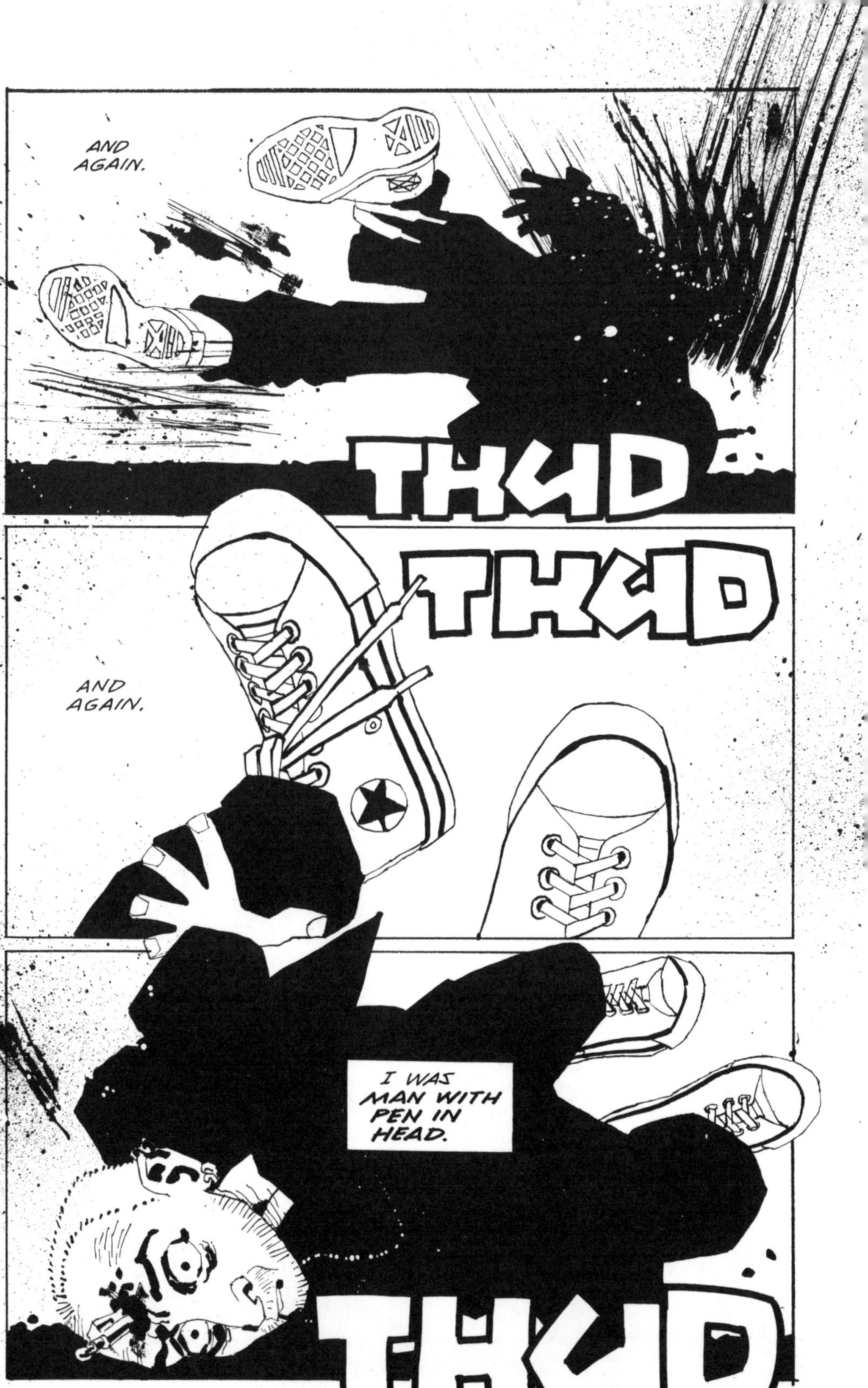
AND AGAIN.
THUD
THUD
AND AGAIN.
I WAS MAN WITH PEN IN HEAD.
THUD

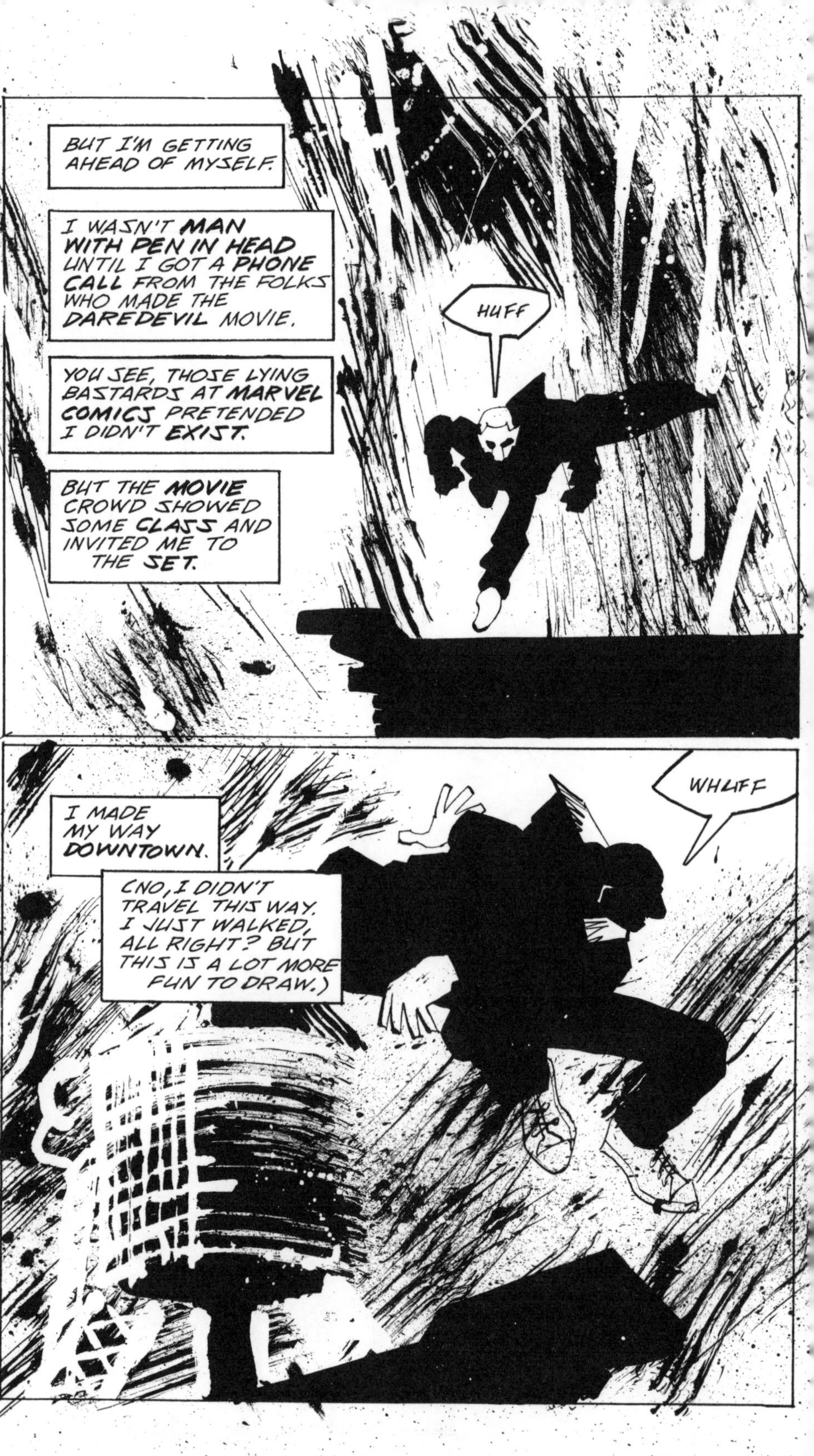
BUT I'M GETTING AHEAD OF MYSELF.
I WASN'T MAN WITH PEN IN HEAD UNTIL I GOT A PHONE CALL FROM THE FOLKS WHO MADE THE DAREDEVIL MOVIE.
YOU SEE, THOSE LYING BASTARDS AT MARVEL COMICS PRETENDED I DIDN'T EXIST.
BUT THE MOVIE CROWD SHOWED SOME CLASS AND INVITED ME TO THE SET.
HUFF
I MADE MY WAY DOWNTOWN.
(NO, I DIDN'T TRAVEL THIS WAY. I JUST WALKED, ALL RIGHT? BUT THIS IS A LOT MORE FUN TO DRAW.)
WHUFF

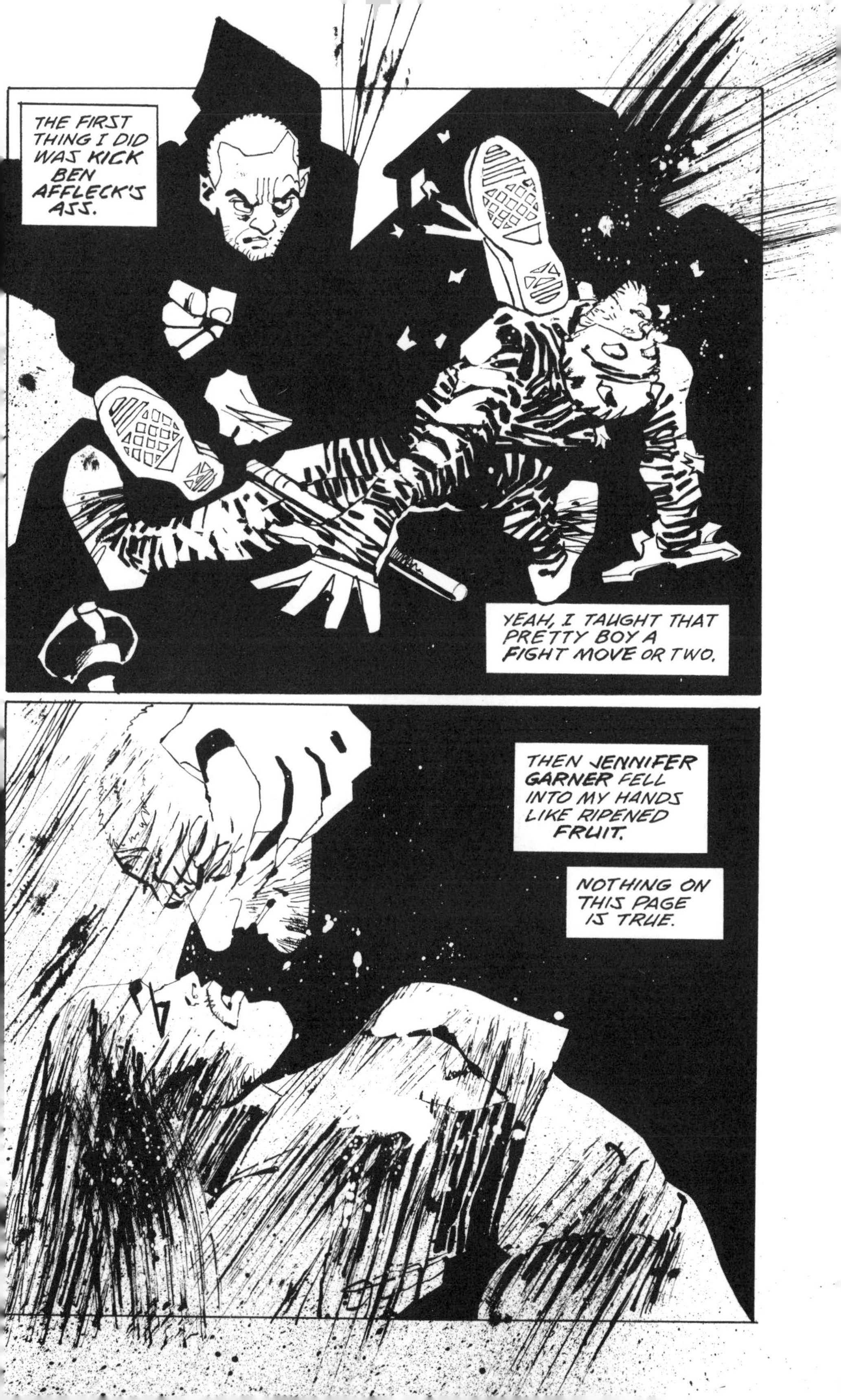
THE FIRST THING I DID WAS KICK BEN AFFLECK'S ASS.
YEAH, I TAUGHT THAT PRETTY BOY A FIGHT MOVE OR TWO.
THEN JENNIFER GARNER FELL INTO MY HANDS LIKE RIPENED FRUIT.
NOTHING ON THIS PAGE IS TRUE.

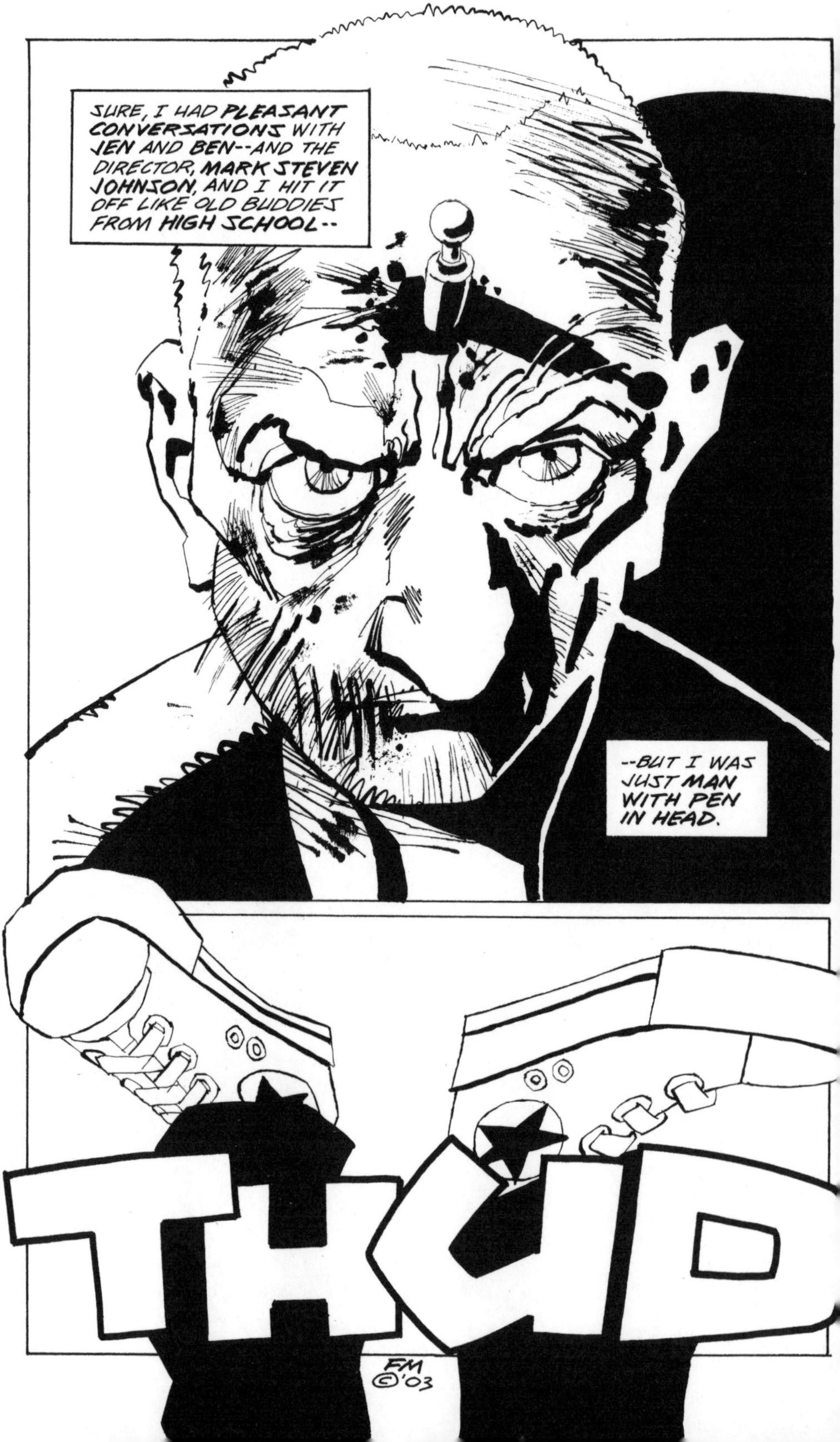
SURE, I HAD PLEASANT CONVERSATIONS WITH JEN AND BEN--AND THE DIRECTOR, MARK STEVEN JOHNSON, AND I HIT IT OFF LIKE OLD BUDDIES FROM HIGH SCHOOL--
--BUT I WAS JUST MAN WITH PEN IN HEAD.
THUD
FM ©'03

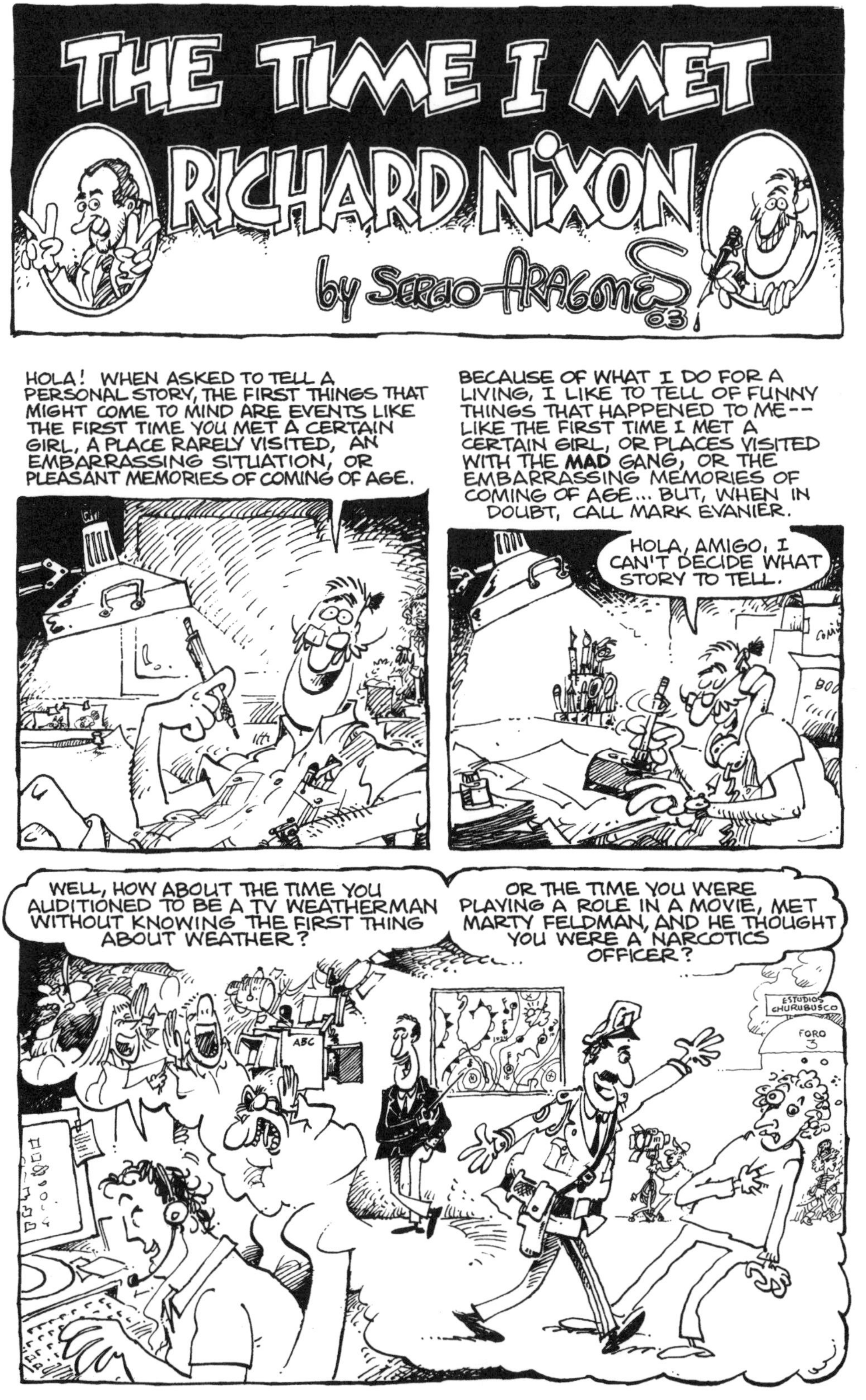
THE TIME I MET RICHARD NIXON
by SERGIO ARAGONÉS 03
HOLA! WHEN ASKED TO TELL A PERSONAL STORY, THE FIRST THINGS THAT MIGHT COME TO MIND ARE EVENTS LIKE THE FIRST TIME YOU MET A CERTAIN GIRL, A PLACE RARELY VISITED, AN EMBARRASSING SITUATION, OR PLEASANT MEMORIES OF COMING OF AGE.
BECAUSE OF WHAT I DO FOR A LIVING, I LIKE TO TELL OF FUNNY THINGS THAT HAPPENED TO ME-- LIKE THE FIRST TIME I MET A CERTAIN GIRL, OR PLACES VISITED WITH THE **MAD** GANG, OR THE EMBARRASSING MEMORIES OF COMING OF AGE... BUT, WHEN IN DOUBT, CALL MARK EVANIER.
HOLA, AMIGO, I CAN'T DECIDE WHAT STORY TO TELL.
WELL, HOW ABOUT THE TIME YOU AUDITIONED TO BE A TV WEATHERMAN WITHOUT KNOWING THE FIRST THING ABOUT WEATHER?
OR THE TIME YOU WERE PLAYING A ROLE IN A MOVIE, MET MARTY FELDMAN, AND HE THOUGHT YOU WERE A NARCOTICS OFFICER?
ABC
ESTUDIOS CHURUBUSCO
FORO 3

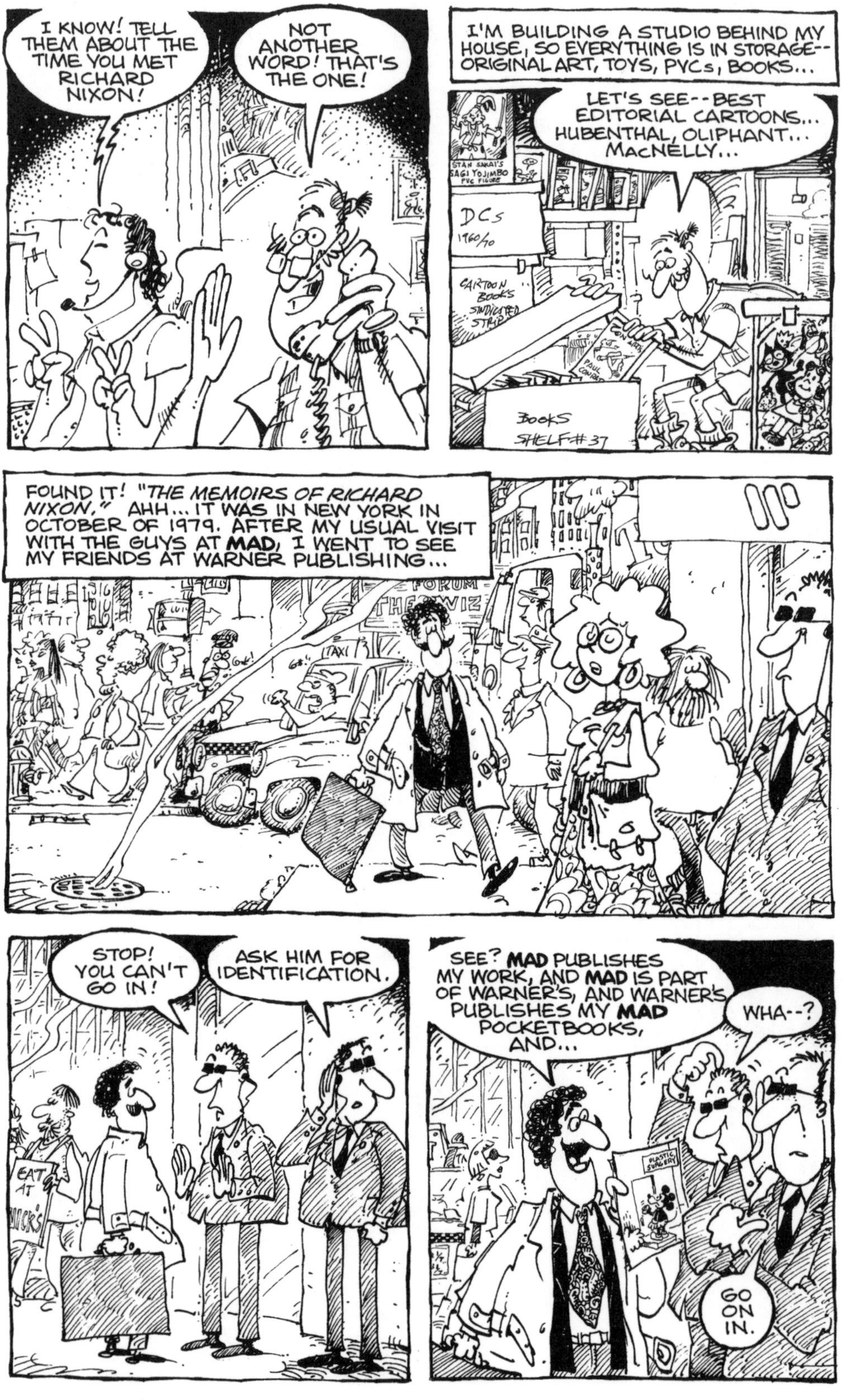

I KNOW! TELL THEM ABOUT THE TIME YOU MET RICHARD NIXON!
NOT ANOTHER WORD! THAT'S THE ONE!
I'M BUILDING A STUDIO BEHIND MY HOUSE, SO EVERYTHING IS IN STORAGE-- ORIGINAL ART, TOYS, PVCs, BOOKS...
LET'S SEE--BEST EDITORIAL CARTOONS... HUBENTHAL, OLIPHANT... MacNELLY...
STAN SAKAI'S USAGI YOJIMBO PVC FIGURE
DCs 1960/70
CARTOON BOOKS
BOOKS SHELF #37
PAUL CONRAD
FOUND IT! *"THE MEMOIRS OF RICHARD NIXON."* AHH... IT WAS IN NEW YORK IN OCTOBER OF 1979. AFTER MY USUAL VISIT WITH THE GUYS AT **MAD**, I WENT TO SEE MY FRIENDS AT WARNER PUBLISHING...
FORUM
THE WIZ
TAXI
STOP! YOU CAN'T GO IN!
ASK HIM FOR IDENTIFICATION.
EAT AT NICK'S
SEE? **MAD** PUBLISHES MY WORK, AND **MAD** IS PART OF WARNER'S, AND WARNER'S PUBLISHES MY **MAD** POCKETBOOKS, AND...
WHA--?
PLASTIC SURGERY
GO ON IN.

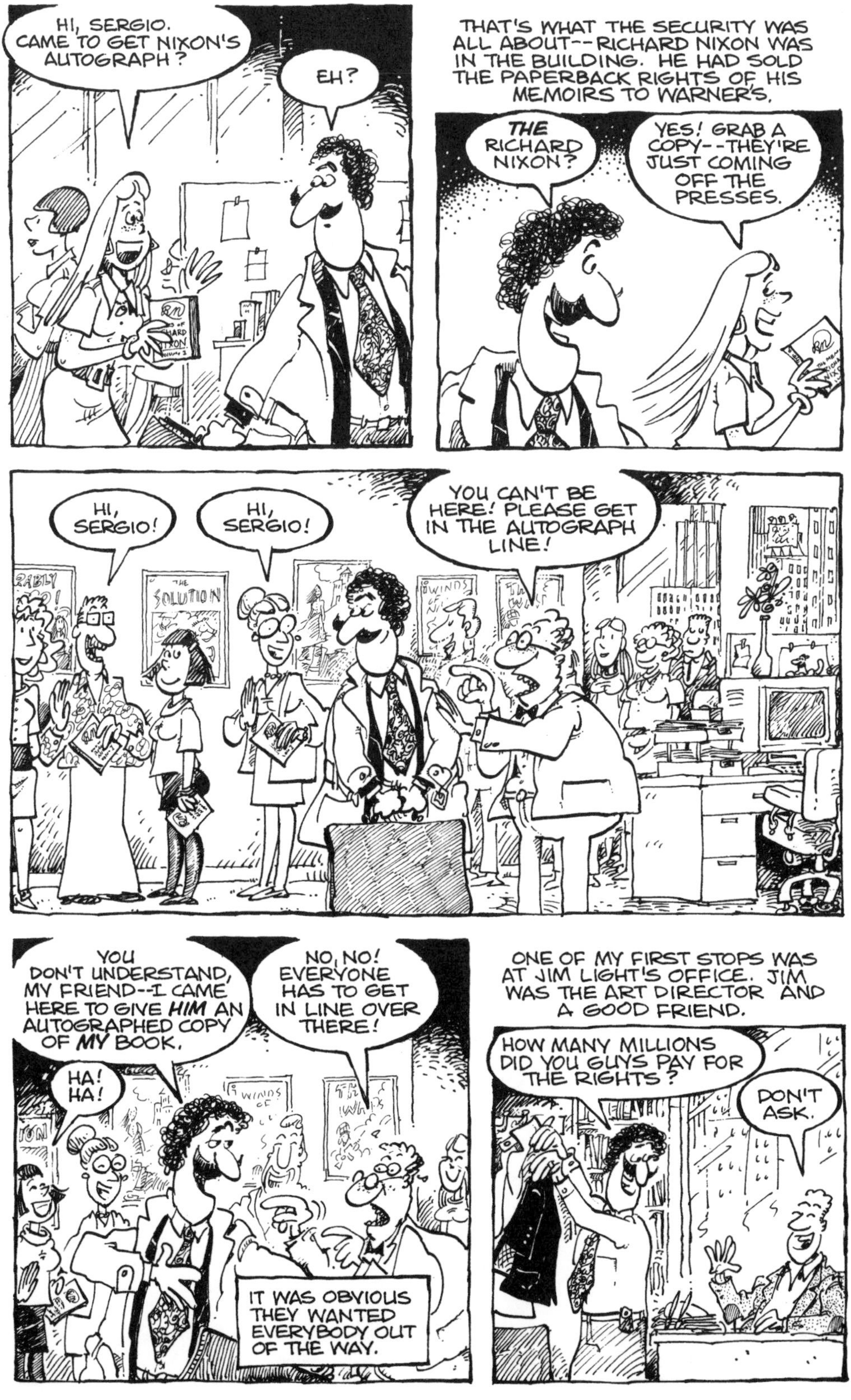
HI, SERGIO. CAME TO GET NIXON'S AUTOGRAPH?
EH?
THAT'S WHAT THE SECURITY WAS ALL ABOUT--RICHARD NIXON WAS IN THE BUILDING. HE HAD SOLD THE PAPERBACK RIGHTS OF HIS MEMOIRS TO WARNER'S.
THE RICHARD NIXON?
YES! GRAB A COPY--THEY'RE JUST COMING OFF THE PRESSES.
HI, SERGIO!
HI, SERGIO!
YOU CAN'T BE HERE! PLEASE GET IN THE AUTOGRAPH LINE!
YOU DON'T UNDERSTAND, MY FRIEND--I CAME HERE TO GIVE HIM AN AUTOGRAPHED COPY OF MY BOOK.
NO, NO! EVERYONE HAS TO GET IN LINE OVER THERE!
HA! HA!
IT WAS OBVIOUS THEY WANTED EVERYBODY OUT OF THE WAY.
ONE OF MY FIRST STOPS WAS AT JIM LIGHT'S OFFICE. JIM WAS THE ART DIRECTOR AND A GOOD FRIEND.
HOW MANY MILLIONS DID YOU GUYS PAY FOR THE RIGHTS?
DON'T ASK.

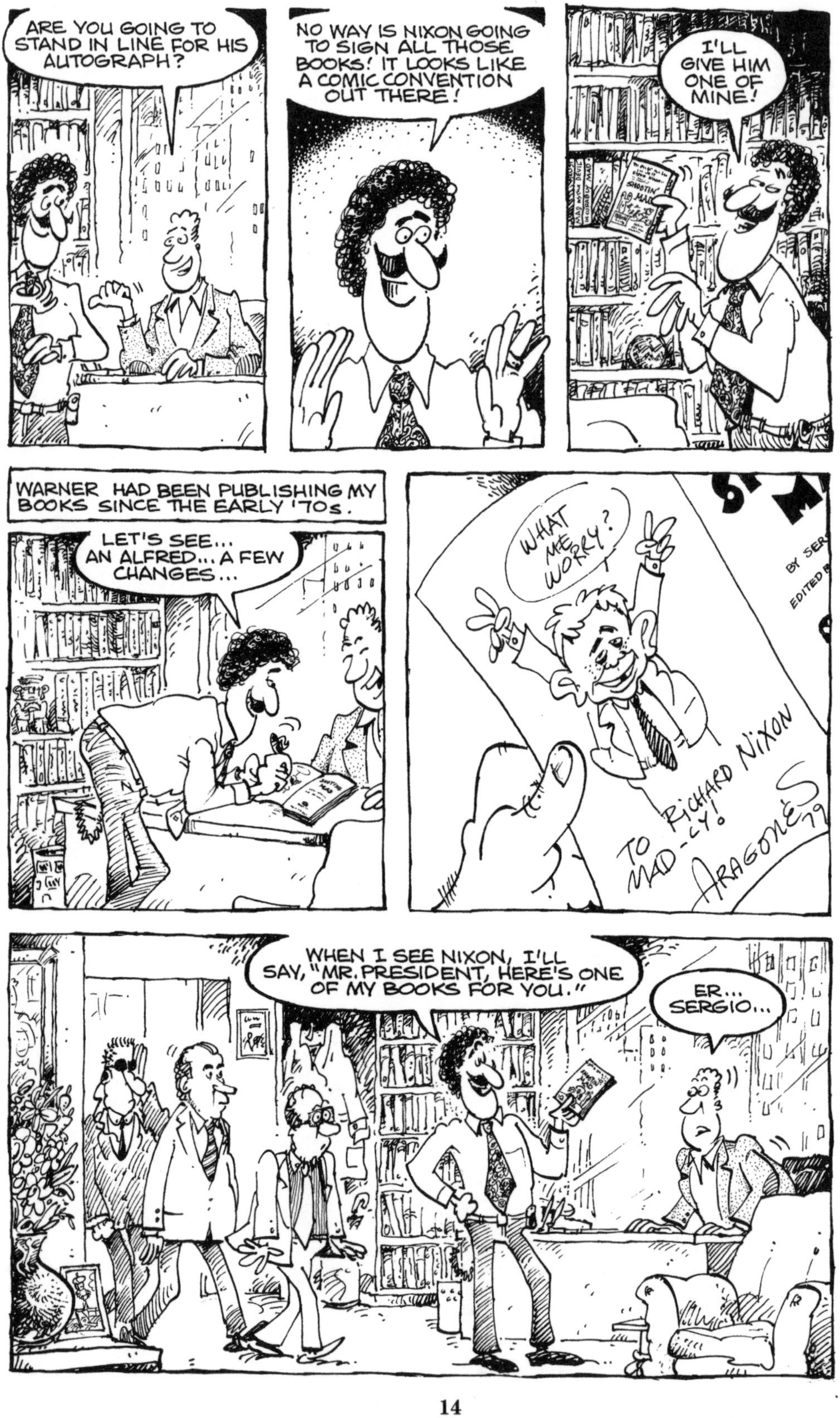
ARE YOU GOING TO STAND IN LINE FOR HIS AUTOGRAPH?
NO WAY IS NIXON GOING TO SIGN ALL THOSE BOOKS! IT LOOKS LIKE A COMIC CONVENTION OUT THERE!
I'LL GIVE HIM ONE OF MINE!
WARNER HAD BEEN PUBLISHING MY BOOKS SINCE THE EARLY '70s.
LET'S SEE... AN ALFRED... A FEW CHANGES...
WHAT ME WORRY?
TO RICHARD NIXON
MAD-CY!
ARAGONÉS 79
WHEN I SEE NIXON, I'LL SAY, "MR. PRESIDENT, HERE'S ONE OF MY BOOKS FOR YOU."
ER... SERGIO...

15

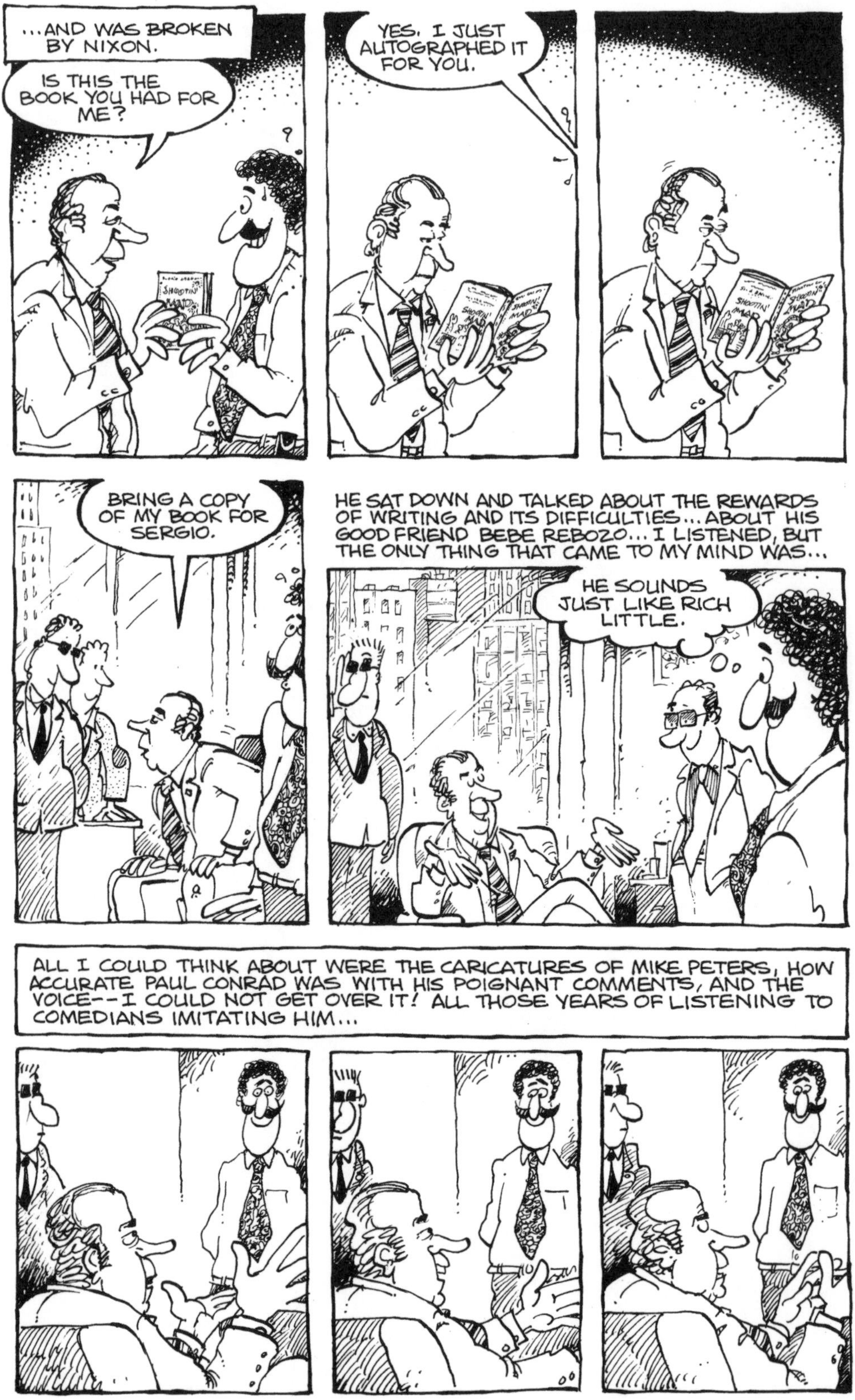
...AND WAS BROKEN BY NIXON.
IS THIS THE BOOK YOU HAD FOR ME?
YES. I JUST AUTOGRAPHED IT FOR YOU.
BRING A COPY OF MY BOOK FOR SERGIO.
HE SAT DOWN AND TALKED ABOUT THE REWARDS OF WRITING AND ITS DIFFICULTIES... ABOUT HIS GOOD FRIEND BEBE REBOZO... I LISTENED, BUT THE ONLY THING THAT CAME TO MY MIND WAS...
HE SOUNDS JUST LIKE RICH LITTLE.
ALL I COULD THINK ABOUT WERE THE CARICATURES OF MIKE PETERS, HOW ACCURATE PAUL CONRAD WAS WITH HIS POIGNANT COMMENTS, AND THE VOICE--I COULD NOT GET OVER IT! ALL THOSE YEARS OF LISTENING TO COMEDIANS IMITATING HIM...

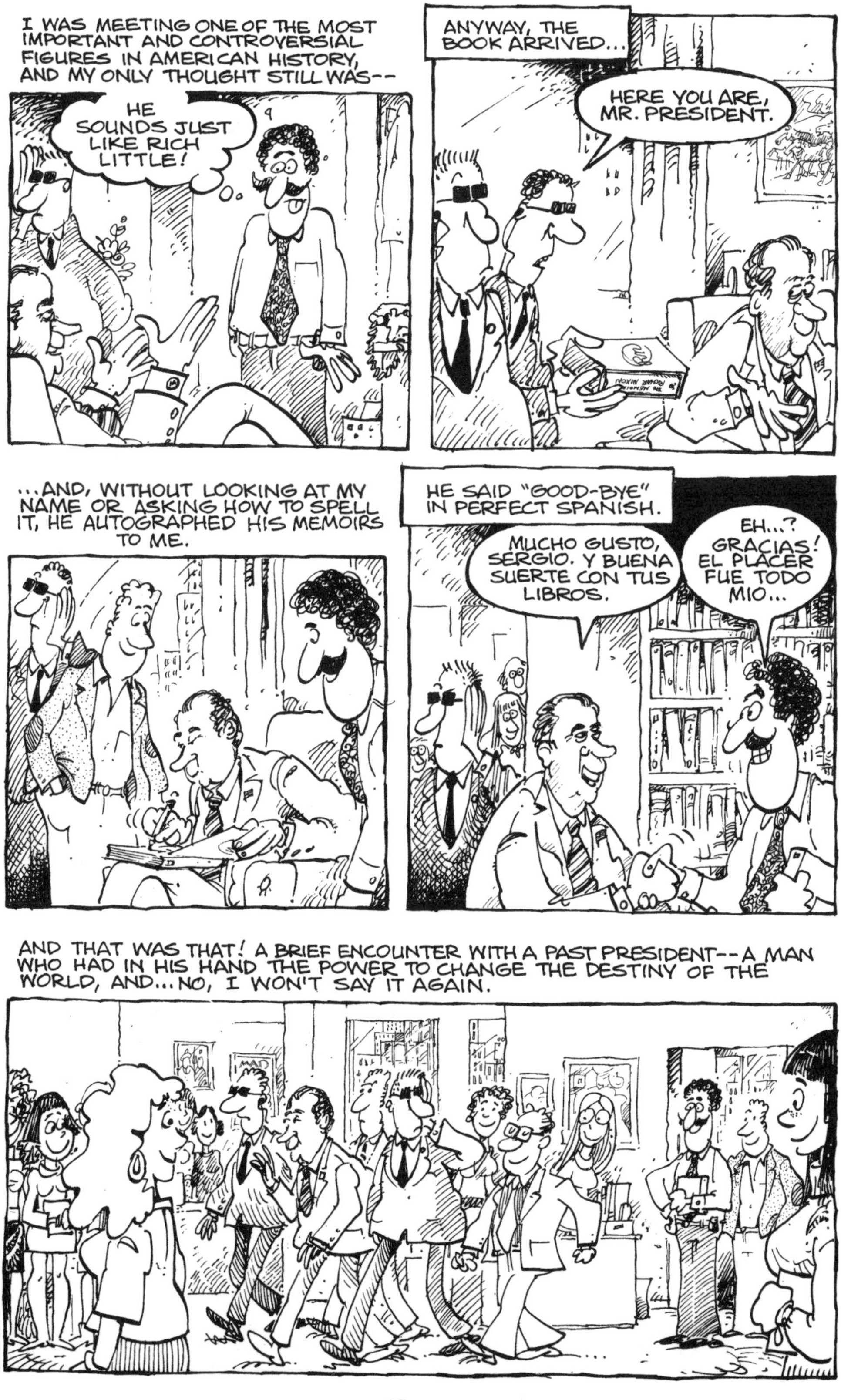
I WAS MEETING ONE OF THE MOST IMPORTANT AND CONTROVERSIAL FIGURES IN AMERICAN HISTORY, AND MY ONLY THOUGHT STILL WAS--
HE SOUNDS JUST LIKE RICH LITTLE!
ANYWAY, THE BOOK ARRIVED...
HERE YOU ARE, MR. PRESIDENT.
...AND, WITHOUT LOOKING AT MY NAME OR ASKING HOW TO SPELL IT, HE AUTOGRAPHED HIS MEMOIRS TO ME.
HE SAID "GOOD-BYE" IN PERFECT SPANISH.
MUCHO GUSTO, SERGIO. Y BUENA SUERTE CON TUS LIBROS.
EH...? GRACIAS! EL PLACER FUE TODO MIO...
AND THAT WAS THAT! A BRIEF ENCOUNTER WITH A PAST PRESIDENT--A MAN WHO HAD IN HIS HAND THE POWER TO CHANGE THE DESTINY OF THE WORLD, AND...NO, I WON'T SAY IT AGAIN.

18

THE DAY I BECAME A PROFESSIONAL

BY Will Eisner

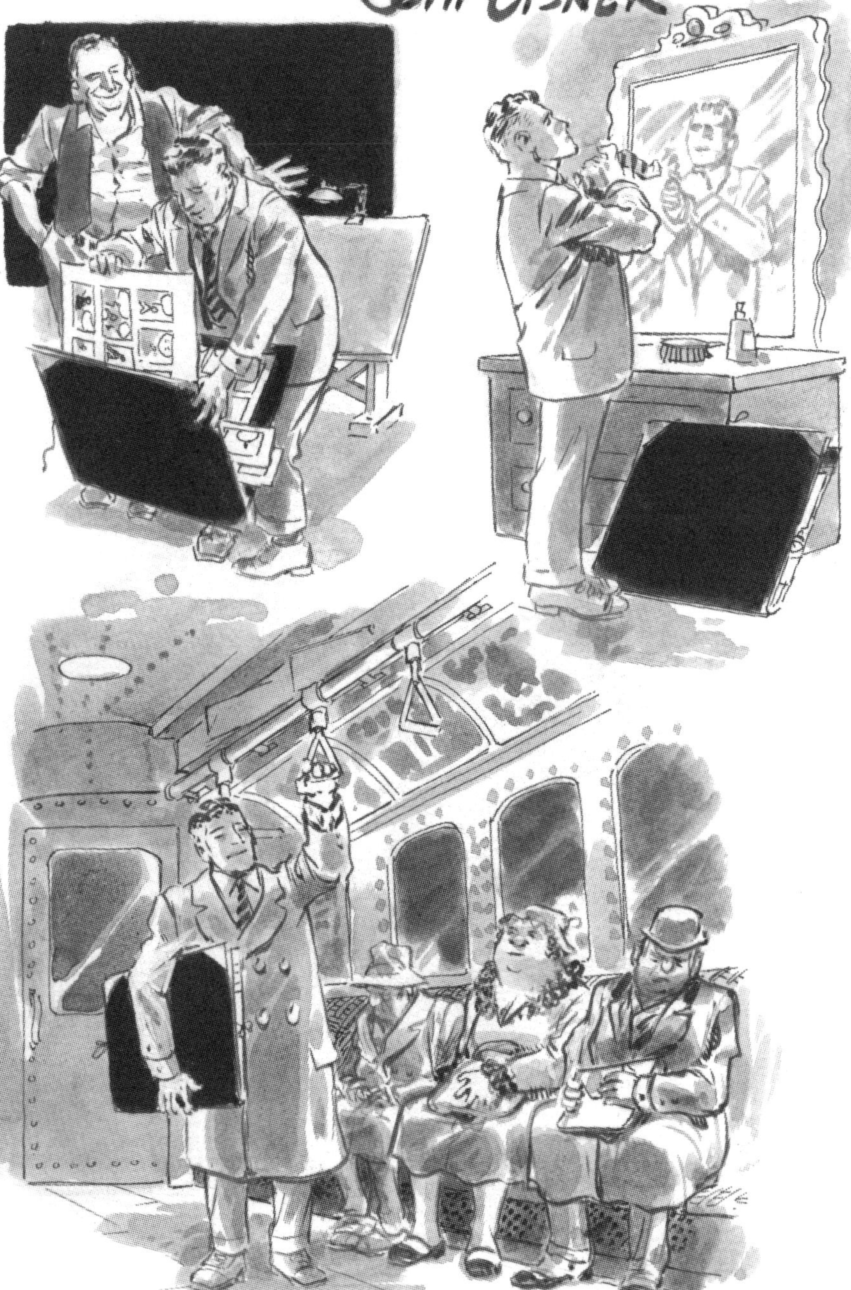

* LUDWIG BEMELMANS, 1898-1962, ACCLAIMED PAINTER, FAMOUS AUTHOR AND ILLUSTRATOR OF CHILDREN'S BOOKS

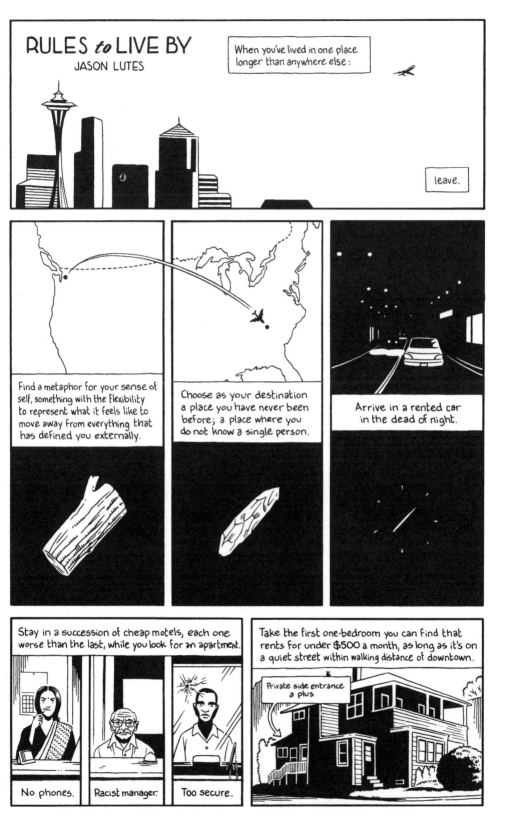

RULES *to* LIVE BY

JASON LUTES

When you've lived in one place longer than anywhere else:

leave.

Find a metaphor for your sense of self, something with the flexibility to represent what it feels like to move away from everything that has defined you externally.

Choose as your destination a place you have never been before; a place where you do not know a single person.

Arrive in a rented car in the dead of night.

Stay in a succession of cheap motels, each one worse than the last, while you look for an apartment.

No phones.

Racist manager.

Too secure.

Take the first one-bedroom you can find that rents for under $500 a month, as long as it's on a quiet street within walking distance of downtown.

Private side entrance a plus

A "sense of place" in a story is important to me.

I think that your environment can be as much a part of you as you are a part of it.

But only if you let it. Living here, getting around only on foot or by bike, has made me feel that all the more acutely.

Downtown Asheville, consisting mostly of buildings that date from before the Depression, rests in a sort of protective pocket.

The eastern border is defined by Beaucatcher Mountain, pierced by Beaucatcher Tunnel in 1929.

And on the far side, spreading out along the four lanes of Tunnel Road to the horizon, are the parking lots, chain franchises, and superstores of the Great American Strip.

Walking from downtown out to Tunnel Road is dispiriting, to say the least. The Tunnel was not built for pedestrians, and the traffic is deafening.

The first time I did it, to buy a cheese grater at Wal-Mart, it felt like my own personal descent into Hell.

I tried to see the experience in symbolic terms, to relate it to the fragile state of my psyche, but in the end I had to question the whole idea of using landscape to *represent* something.

THIS *is not a* METAPHOR

25

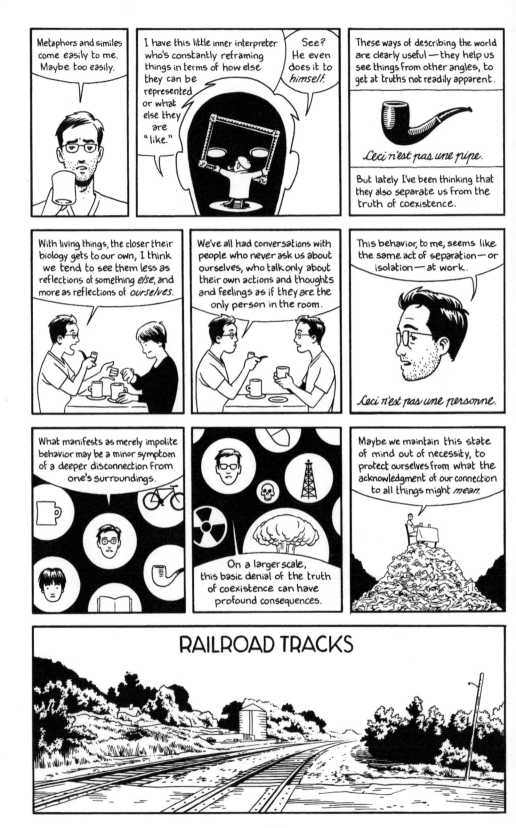

On February 2, 1966, Cleve Backster made a discovery about this basic disconnection that changed his life.

Mr. Backster is a leading polygraph expert. He created the standard test used by lie detection examiners worldwide, and along with running a lab devoted to polygraph science, he trains law enforcement officials in proper use of the device.

On February 2, 1966, he bought a plant for the lab and, after watering it, decided on a whim to see if a polygraph machine attached to the plant would register any change when the water traveled all the way out to the leaves.

LEAF

H_2O

GALVANIC RESPONSE DETECTOR

He was surprised to see something on the chart resembling a human response, and began to wonder if there might be a way to trigger a physiological response in the plant *that* the polygraph could measure.

At 13 minutes, 55 seconds chart time, the imagery entered my mind of burning the leaf.

I didn't verbalize, I didn't touch the plant; I didn't touch the equipment.

The pen jumped right off the top of the chart.

This event altered Mr. Backster's consciousness permanently. From that moment on, he devoted his life to studying the extent and ramifications of what some have termed "bio communication."

Decades of research have led him to believe that, given time, living things can attune themselves to their environment and everything in it, particularly other living things.

He has proven that subjects —plants, yogurt cultures, human cells— register a physiological response when the things to which they are attuned suffer damage, death, or emotional duress.

Instantaneously, at distances of up to 300 miles.

Extrasensory perception?

Primary perception.

a RIVER

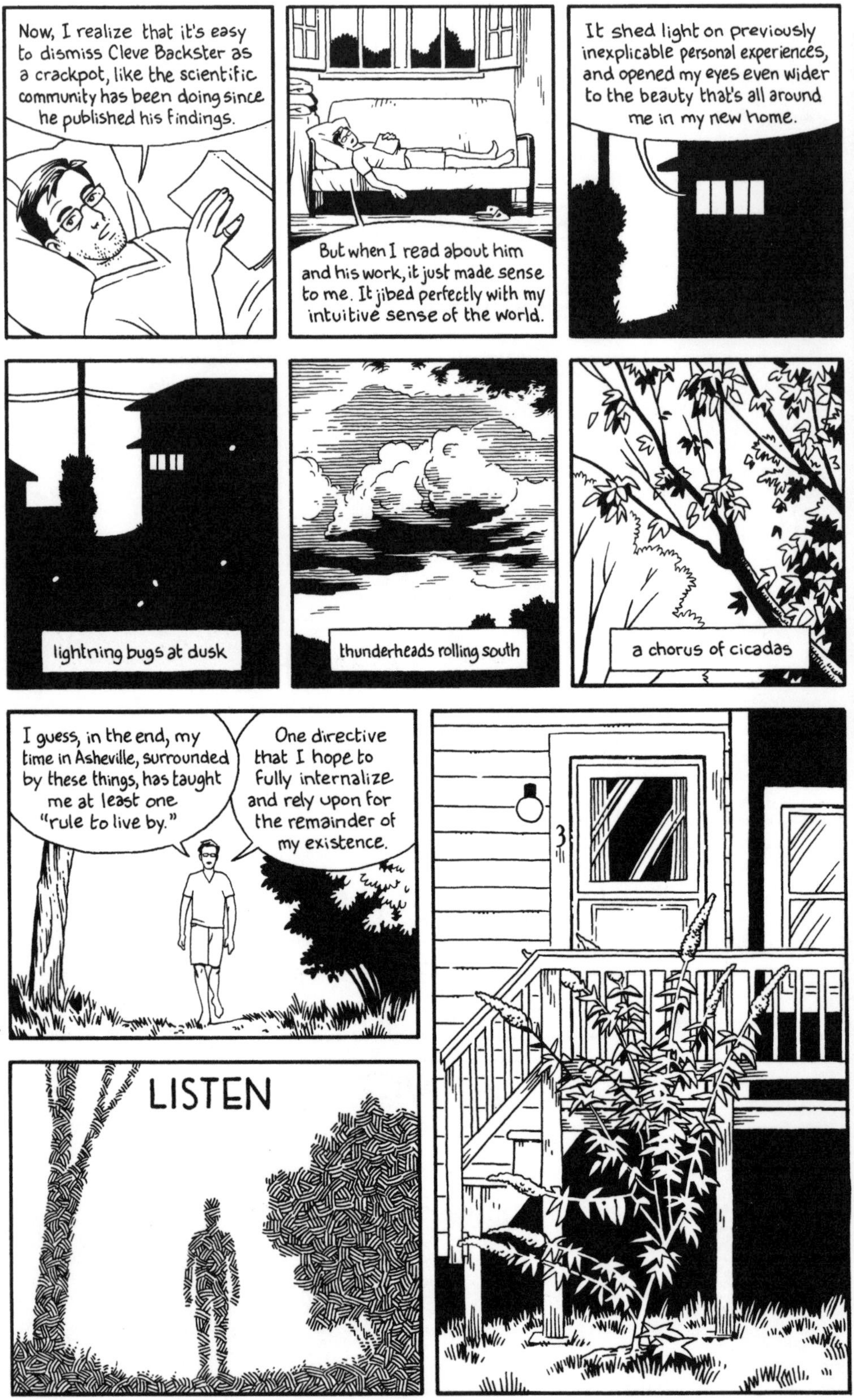
Now, I realize that it's easy to dismiss Cleve Backster as a crackpot, like the scientific community has been doing since he published his findings.
But when I read about him and his work, it just made sense to me. It jibed perfectly with my intuitive sense of the world.
It shed light on previously inexplicable personal experiences, and opened my eyes even wider to the beauty that's all around me in my new home.
lightning bugs at dusk
thunderheads rolling south
a chorus of cicadas
I guess, in the end, my time in Asheville, surrounded by these things, has taught me at least one "rule to live by."
One directive that I hope to fully internalize and rely upon for the remainder of my existence.
LISTEN
3

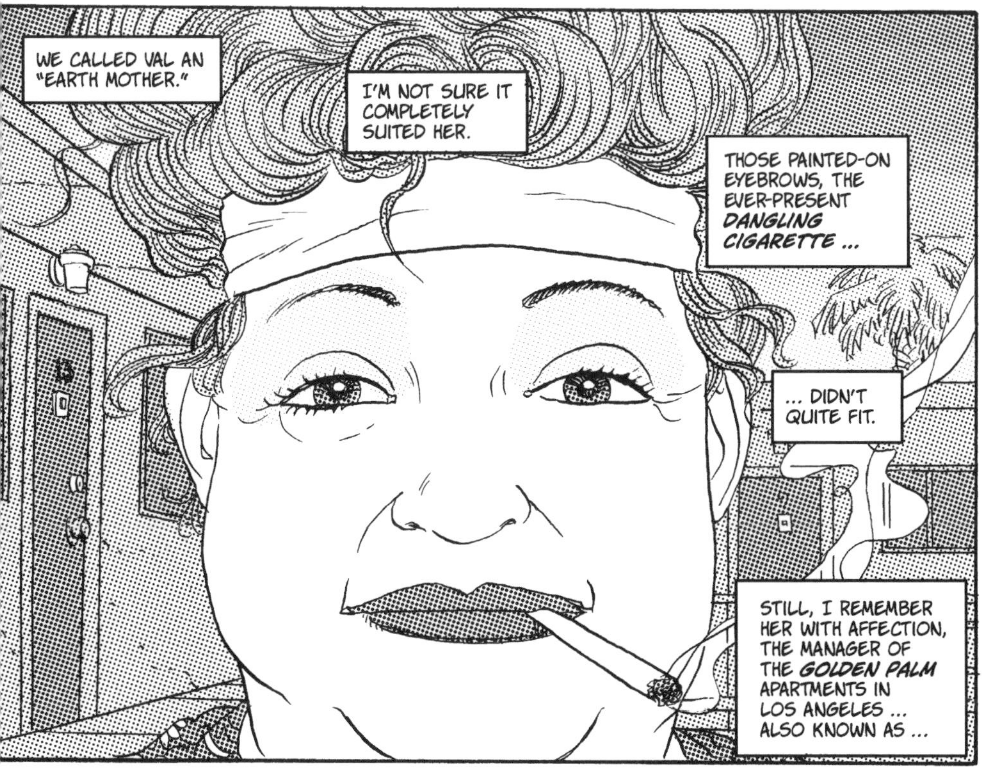
WE CALLED VAL AN "EARTH MOTHER."
I'M NOT SURE IT COMPLETELY SUITED HER.
THOSE PAINTED-ON EYEBROWS, THE EVER-PRESENT DANGLING CIGARETTE ...
... DIDN'T QUITE FIT.
STILL, I REMEMBER HER WITH AFFECTION, THE MANAGER OF THE GOLDEN PALM APARTMENTS IN LOS ANGELES ... ALSO KNOWN AS ...

THE BUILDING THAT DIDN'T EXPLODE

PAUL CHADWICK 2003

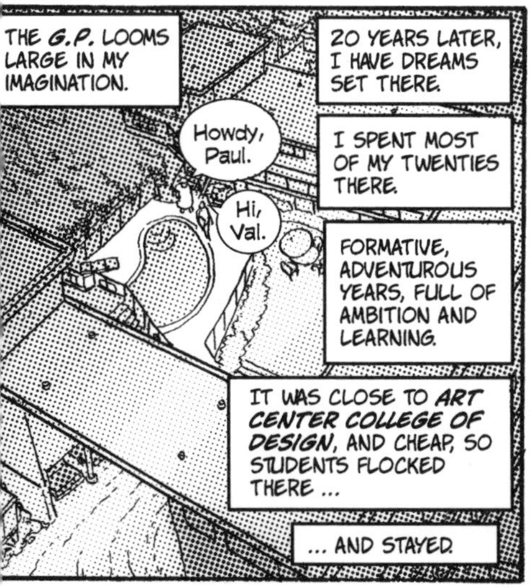
THE G.P. LOOMS LARGE IN MY IMAGINATION.
20 YEARS LATER, I HAVE DREAMS SET THERE.
I SPENT MOST OF MY TWENTIES THERE.
Howdy, Paul.
Hi, Val.
FORMATIVE, ADVENTUROUS YEARS, FULL OF AMBITION AND LEARNING.
IT WAS CLOSE TO ART CENTER COLLEGE OF DESIGN, AND CHEAP, SO STUDENTS FLOCKED THERE ...
... AND STAYED.

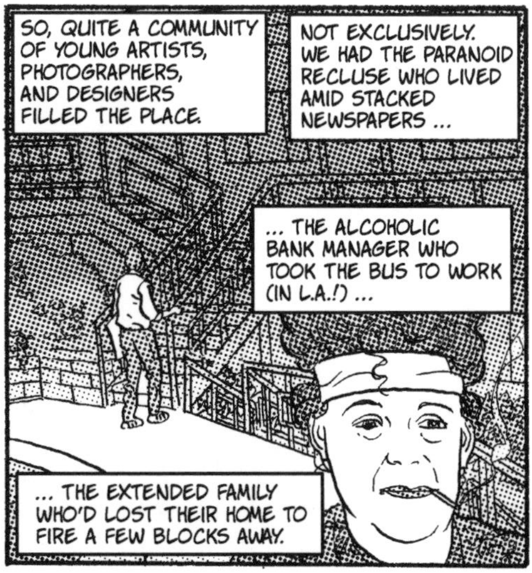
SO, QUITE A COMMUNITY OF YOUNG ARTISTS, PHOTOGRAPHERS, AND DESIGNERS FILLED THE PLACE.
NOT EXCLUSIVELY. WE HAD THE PARANOID RECLUSE WHO LIVED AMID STACKED NEWSPAPERS ...
... THE ALCOHOLIC BANK MANAGER WHO TOOK THE BUS TO WORK (IN L.A.!) ...
... THE EXTENDED FAMILY WHO'D LOST THEIR HOME TO FIRE A FEW BLOCKS AWAY.

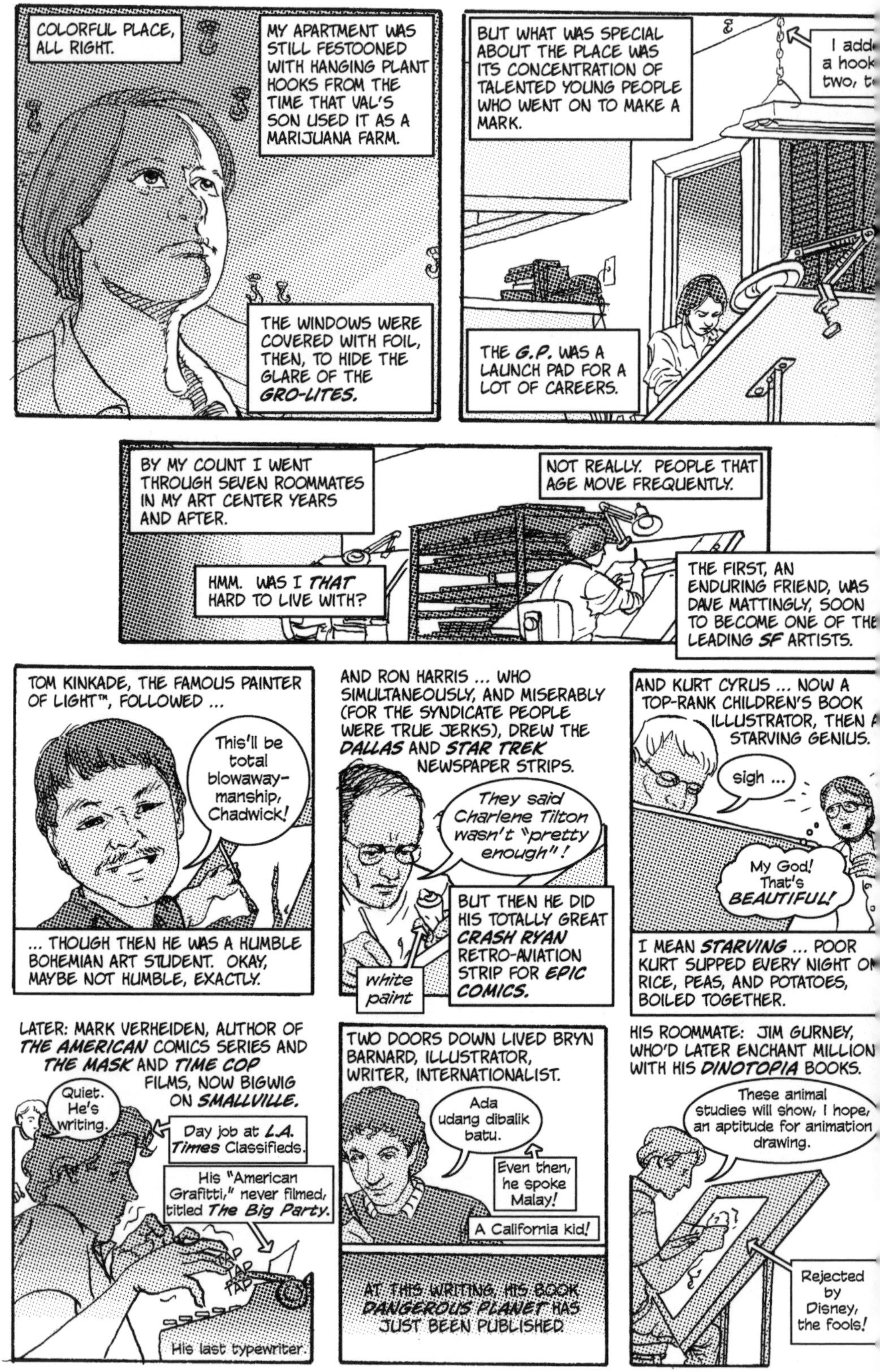
COLORFUL PLACE, ALL RIGHT.
MY APARTMENT WAS STILL FESTOONED WITH HANGING PLANT HOOKS FROM THE TIME THAT VAL'S SON USED IT AS A MARIJUANA FARM.
THE WINDOWS WERE COVERED WITH FOIL, THEN, TO HIDE THE GLARE OF THE *GRO-LITES.*
BUT WHAT WAS SPECIAL ABOUT THE PLACE WAS ITS CONCENTRATION OF TALENTED YOUNG PEOPLE WHO WENT ON TO MAKE A MARK.
I add a hook two, t
THE *G.P.* WAS A LAUNCH PAD FOR A LOT OF CAREERS.
BY MY COUNT I WENT THROUGH SEVEN ROOMMATES IN MY ART CENTER YEARS AND AFTER.
NOT REALLY. PEOPLE THAT AGE MOVE FREQUENTLY.
HMM. WAS I *THAT* HARD TO LIVE WITH?
THE FIRST, AN ENDURING FRIEND, WAS DAVE MATTINGLY, SOON TO BECOME ONE OF THE LEADING *SF* ARTISTS.
TOM KINKADE, THE FAMOUS PAINTER OF LIGHT™, FOLLOWED ...
This'll be total blowaway-manship, Chadwick!
... THOUGH THEN HE WAS A HUMBLE BOHEMIAN ART STUDENT. OKAY, MAYBE NOT HUMBLE, EXACTLY.
AND RON HARRIS ... WHO SIMULTANEOUSLY, AND MISERABLY (FOR THE SYNDICATE PEOPLE WERE TRUE JERKS), DREW THE *DALLAS* AND *STAR TREK* NEWSPAPER STRIPS.
They said Charlene Tilton wasn't "pretty enough"!
BUT THEN HE DID HIS TOTALLY GREAT *CRASH RYAN* RETRO-AVIATION STRIP FOR *EPIC COMICS.*
white paint
AND KURT CYRUS ... NOW A TOP-RANK CHILDREN'S BOOK ILLUSTRATOR, THEN A STARVING GENIUS.
sigh ...
My God! That's *BEAUTIFUL!*
I MEAN *STARVING* ... POOR KURT SUPPED EVERY NIGHT ON RICE, PEAS, AND POTATOES, BOILED TOGETHER.
LATER: MARK VERHEIDEN, AUTHOR OF *THE AMERICAN* COMICS SERIES AND *THE MASK* AND *TIME COP* FILMS, NOW BIGWIG ON *SMALLVILLE.*
Quiet. He's writing.
Day job at *L.A. Times* Classifieds.
His "American Grafitti," never filmed, titled *The Big Party.*
TAP TAP
His last typewriter.
TWO DOORS DOWN LIVED BRYN BARNARD, ILLUSTRATOR, WRITER, INTERNATIONALIST.
Ada udang dibalik batu.
Even then, he spoke Malay!
A California kid!
AT THIS WRITING HIS BOOK *DANGEROUS PLANET* HAS JUST BEEN PUBLISHED.
HIS ROOMMATE: JIM GURNEY, WHO'D LATER ENCHANT MILLIONS WITH HIS *DINOTOPIA* BOOKS.
These animal studies will show, I hope, an aptitude for animation drawing.
Rejected by Disney, the fools!

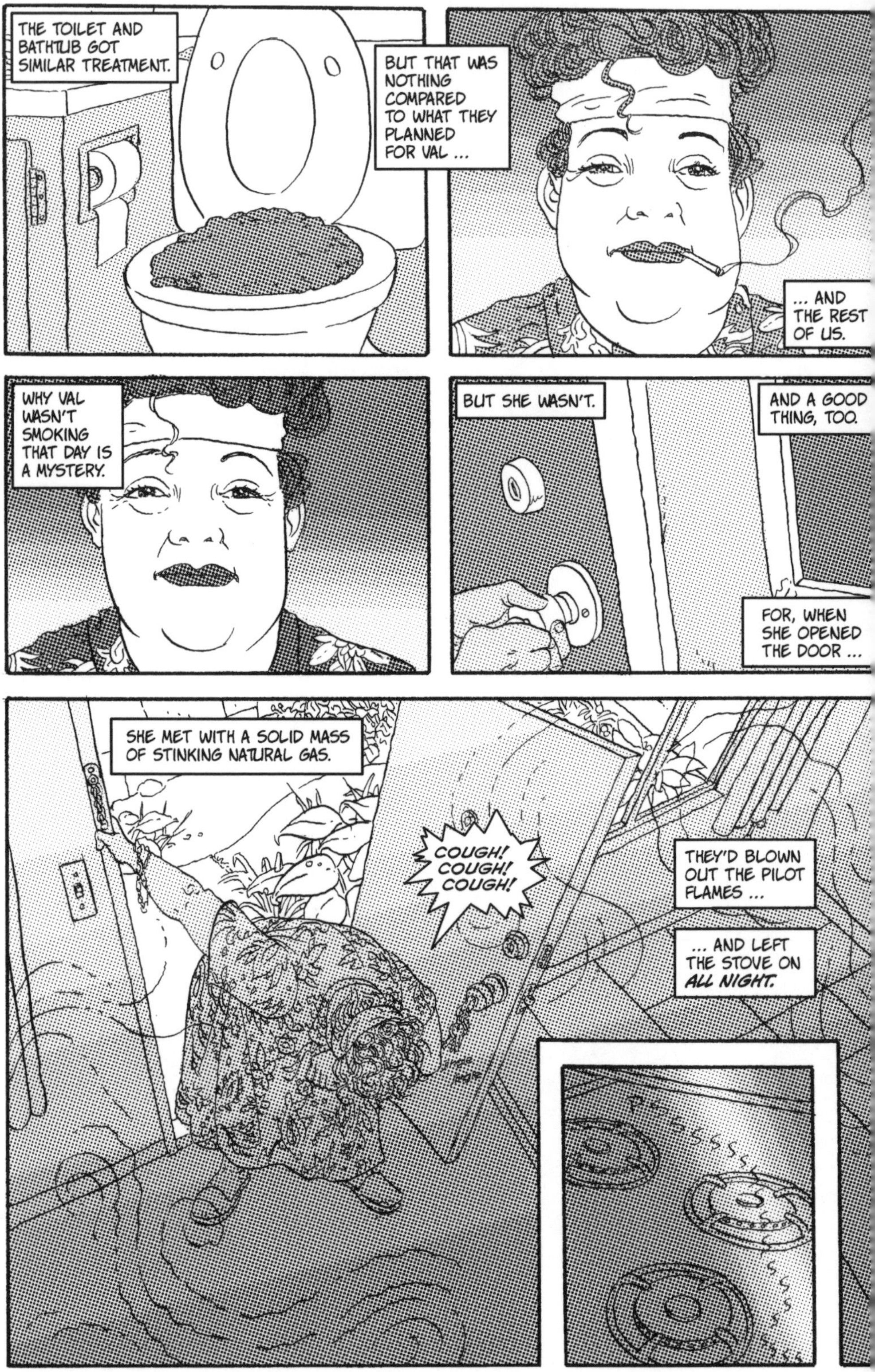
THE TOILET AND BATHTUB GOT SIMILAR TREATMENT.
BUT THAT WAS NOTHING COMPARED TO WHAT THEY PLANNED FOR VAL ...
... AND THE REST OF US.
WHY VAL WASN'T SMOKING THAT DAY IS A MYSTERY.
BUT SHE WASN'T.
AND A GOOD THING, TOO.
FOR, WHEN SHE OPENED THE DOOR ...
SHE MET WITH A SOLID MASS OF STINKING NATURAL GAS.
COUGH! COUGH! COUGH!
THEY'D BLOWN OUT THE PILOT FLAMES ...
... AND LEFT THE STOVE ON *ALL NIGHT.*
PSSSSSS

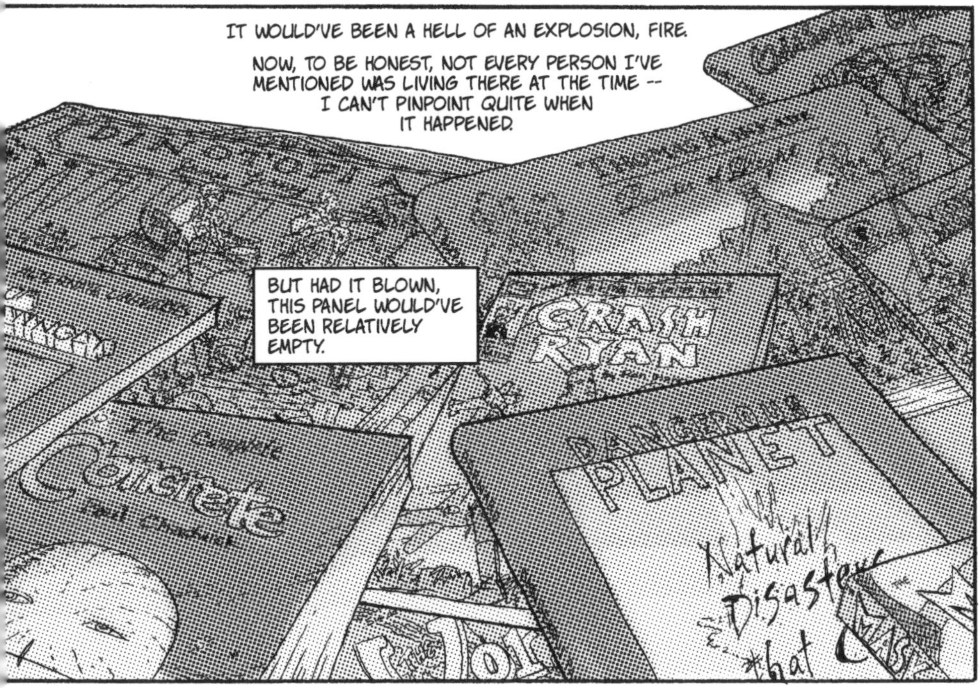

IT WOULD'VE BEEN A HELL OF AN EXPLOSION, FIRE.
NOW, TO BE HONEST, NOT EVERY PERSON I'VE MENTIONED WAS LIVING THERE AT THE TIME -- I CAN'T PINPOINT QUITE WHEN IT HAPPENED.
BUT HAD IT BLOWN, THIS PANEL WOULD'VE BEEN RELATIVELY EMPTY.
CRASH RYAN
The Complete
Concrete
Paul Chadwick
DANGEROUS
PLANET

THE VERY HUMAN QUESTION TO ASK IS: WHY WERE WE SPARED?

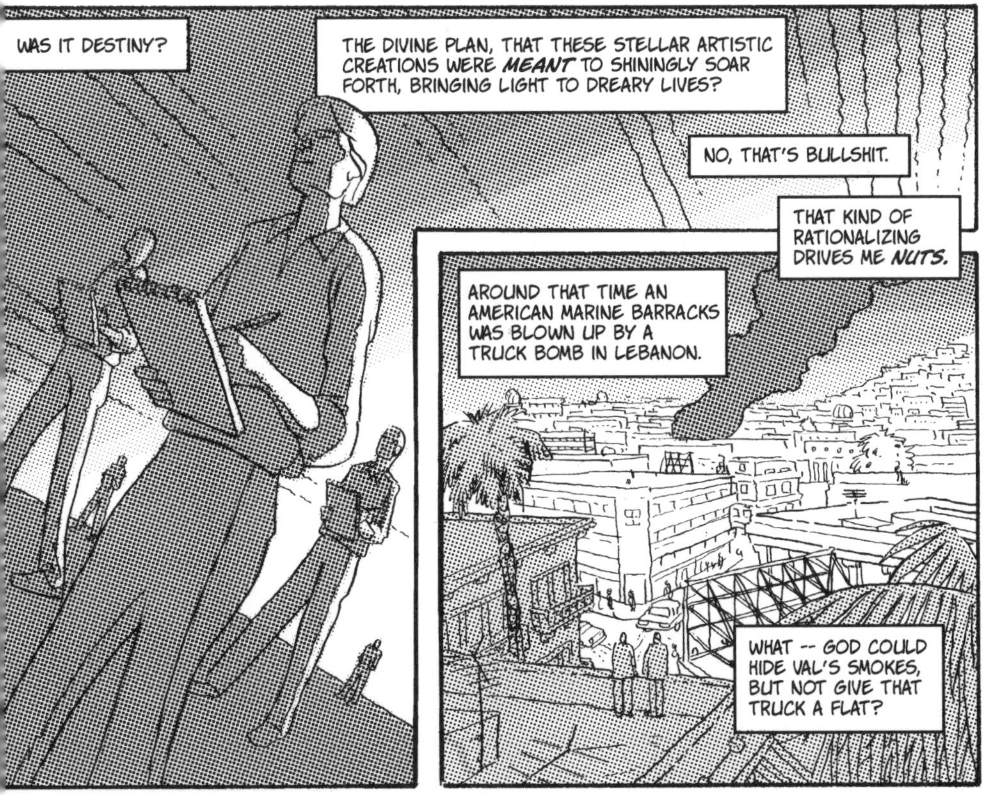

WAS IT DESTINY?
THE DIVINE PLAN, THAT THESE STELLAR ARTISTIC CREATIONS WERE *MEANT* TO SHININGLY SOAR FORTH, BRINGING LIGHT TO DREARY LIVES?
NO, THAT'S BULLSHIT.
THAT KIND OF RATIONALIZING DRIVES ME *NUTS.*
AROUND THAT TIME AN AMERICAN MARINE BARRACKS WAS BLOWN UP BY A TRUCK BOMB IN LEBANON.
WHAT -- GOD COULD HIDE VAL'S SMOKES, BUT NOT GIVE THAT TRUCK A FLAT?

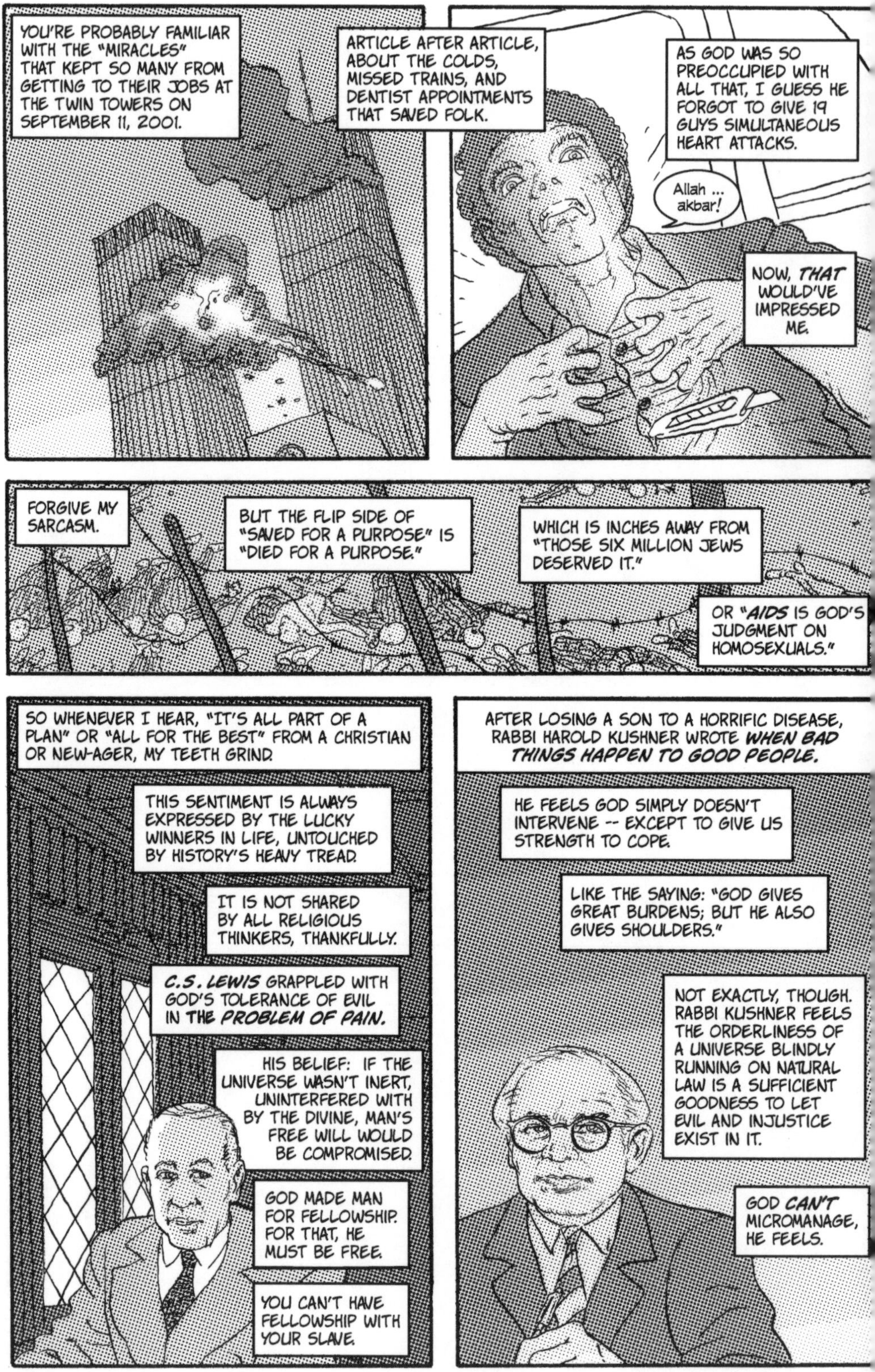
YOU'RE PROBABLY FAMILIAR WITH THE "MIRACLES" THAT KEPT SO MANY FROM GETTING TO THEIR JOBS AT THE TWIN TOWERS ON SEPTEMBER 11, 2001.
ARTICLE AFTER ARTICLE, ABOUT THE COLDS, MISSED TRAINS, AND DENTIST APPOINTMENTS THAT SAVED FOLK.
AS GOD WAS SO PREOCCUPIED WITH ALL THAT, I GUESS HE FORGOT TO GIVE 19 GUYS SIMULTANEOUS HEART ATTACKS.
Allah ... akbar!
NOW, THAT WOULD'VE IMPRESSED ME.
FORGIVE MY SARCASM.
BUT THE FLIP SIDE OF "SAVED FOR A PURPOSE" IS "DIED FOR A PURPOSE."
WHICH IS INCHES AWAY FROM "THOSE SIX MILLION JEWS DESERVED IT."
OR "AIDS IS GOD'S JUDGMENT ON HOMOSEXUALS."
SO WHENEVER I HEAR, "IT'S ALL PART OF A PLAN" OR "ALL FOR THE BEST" FROM A CHRISTIAN OR NEW-AGER, MY TEETH GRIND.
THIS SENTIMENT IS ALWAYS EXPRESSED BY THE LUCKY WINNERS IN LIFE, UNTOUCHED BY HISTORY'S HEAVY TREAD.
IT IS NOT SHARED BY ALL RELIGIOUS THINKERS, THANKFULLY.
C.S. LEWIS GRAPPLED WITH GOD'S TOLERANCE OF EVIL IN THE PROBLEM OF PAIN.
HIS BELIEF: IF THE UNIVERSE WASN'T INERT, UNINTERFERED WITH BY THE DIVINE, MAN'S FREE WILL WOULD BE COMPROMISED.
GOD MADE MAN FOR FELLOWSHIP. FOR THAT, HE MUST BE FREE.
YOU CAN'T HAVE FELLOWSHIP WITH YOUR SLAVE.
AFTER LOSING A SON TO A HORRIFIC DISEASE, RABBI HAROLD KUSHNER WROTE WHEN BAD THINGS HAPPEN TO GOOD PEOPLE.
HE FEELS GOD SIMPLY DOESN'T INTERVENE -- EXCEPT TO GIVE US STRENGTH TO COPE.
LIKE THE SAYING: "GOD GIVES GREAT BURDENS; BUT HE ALSO GIVES SHOULDERS."
NOT EXACTLY, THOUGH. RABBI KUSHNER FEELS THE ORDERLINESS OF A UNIVERSE BLINDLY RUNNING ON NATURAL LAW IS A SUFFICIENT GOODNESS TO LET EVIL AND INJUSTICE EXIST IN IT.
GOD CAN'T MICROMANAGE, HE FEELS.

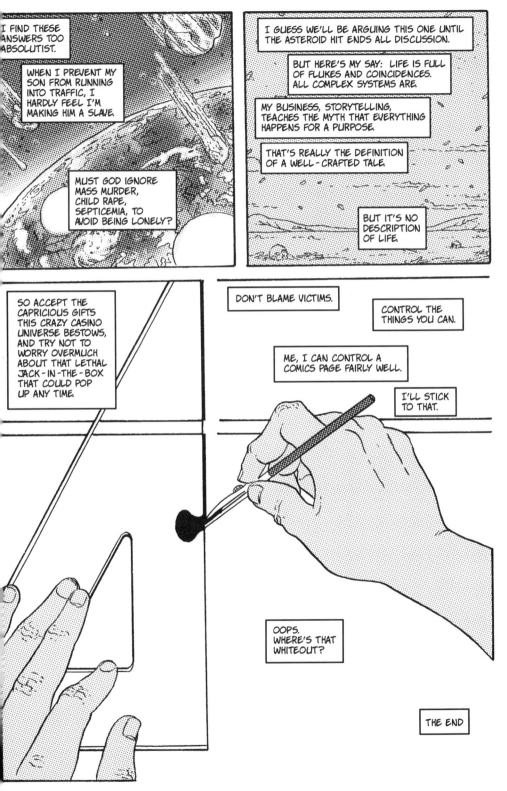

I FIND THESE ANSWERS TOO ABSOLUTIST.

WHEN I PREVENT MY SON FROM RUNNING INTO TRAFFIC, I HARDLY FEEL I'M MAKING HIM A SLAVE.

MUST GOD IGNORE MASS MURDER, CHILD RAPE, SEPTICEMIA, TO AVOID BEING LONELY?

I GUESS WE'LL BE ARGUING THIS ONE UNTIL THE ASTEROID HIT ENDS ALL DISCUSSION.

BUT HERE'S MY SAY: LIFE IS FULL OF FLUKES AND COINCIDENCES. ALL COMPLEX SYSTEMS ARE.

MY BUSINESS, STORYTELLING, TEACHES THE MYTH THAT EVERYTHING HAPPENS FOR A PURPOSE.

THAT'S REALLY THE DEFINITION OF A WELL-CRAFTED TALE.

BUT IT'S NO DESCRIPTION OF LIFE.

SO ACCEPT THE CAPRICIOUS GIFTS THIS CRAZY CASINO UNIVERSE BESTOWS, AND TRY NOT TO WORRY OVERMUCH ABOUT THAT LETHAL JACK-IN-THE-BOX THAT COULD POP UP ANY TIME.

DON'T BLAME VICTIMS.

CONTROL THE THINGS YOU CAN.

ME, I CAN CONTROL A COMICS PAGE FAIRLY WELL.

I'LL STICK TO THAT.

OOPS. WHERE'S THAT WHITEOUT?

THE END

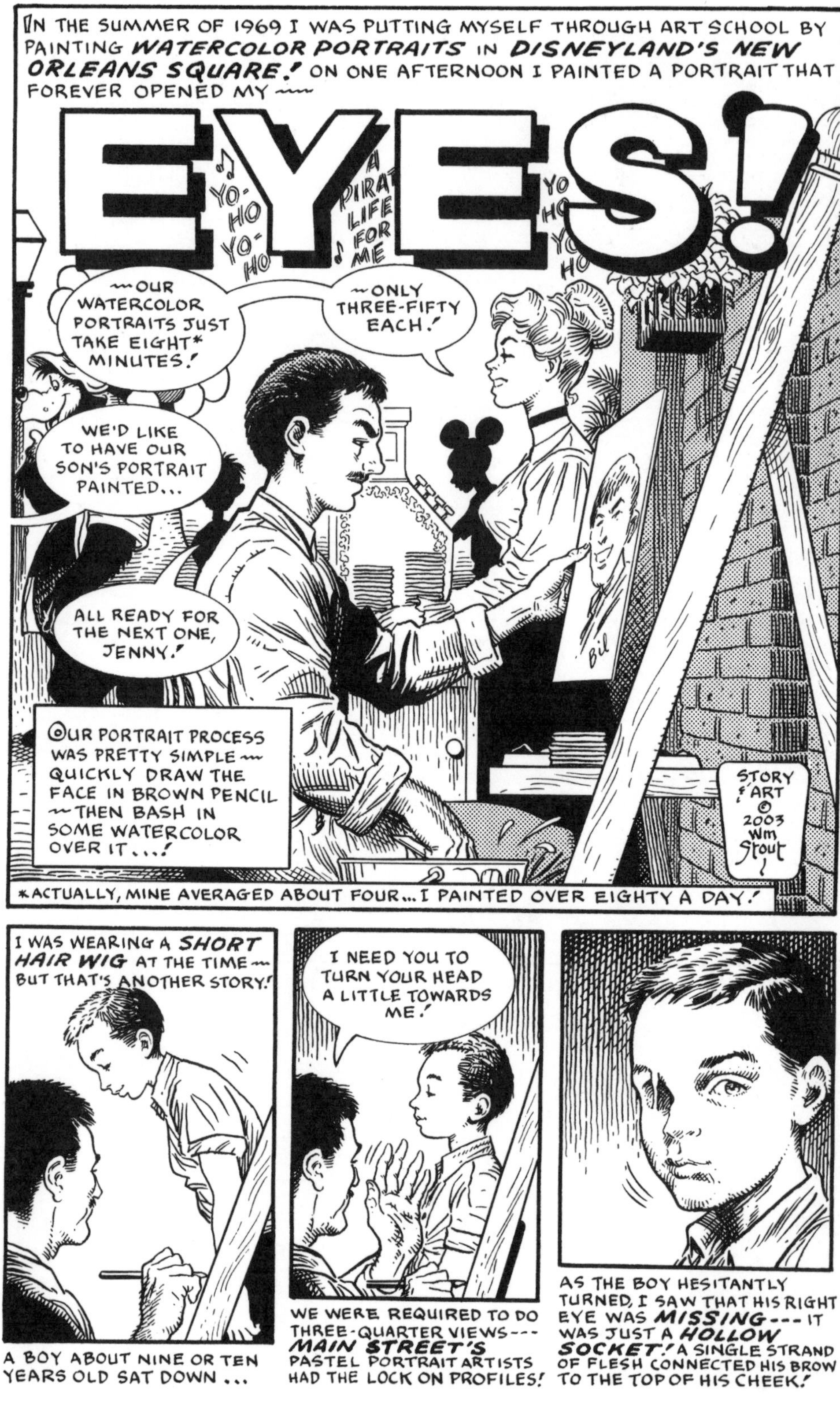
IN THE SUMMER OF 1969 I WAS PUTTING MYSELF THROUGH ART SCHOOL BY PAINTING WATERCOLOR PORTRAITS IN DISNEYLAND'S NEW ORLEANS SQUARE! ON ONE AFTERNOON I PAINTED A PORTRAIT THAT FOREVER OPENED MY ~~
EYES!
YO-HO YO-HO
A PIRAT LIFE FOR ME
YO HO YO HO
~OUR WATERCOLOR PORTRAITS JUST TAKE EIGHT* MINUTES!
~ONLY THREE-FIFTY EACH!
WE'D LIKE TO HAVE OUR SON'S PORTRAIT PAINTED...
ALL READY FOR THE NEXT ONE, JENNY!
Bil
OUR PORTRAIT PROCESS WAS PRETTY SIMPLE ~ QUICKLY DRAW THE FACE IN BROWN PENCIL ~ THEN BASH IN SOME WATERCOLOR OVER IT...!
STORY & ART © 2003 Wm Stout
*ACTUALLY, MINE AVERAGED ABOUT FOUR... I PAINTED OVER EIGHTY A DAY!
I WAS WEARING A SHORT HAIR WIG AT THE TIME ~ BUT THAT'S ANOTHER STORY!
A BOY ABOUT NINE OR TEN YEARS OLD SAT DOWN...
I NEED YOU TO TURN YOUR HEAD A LITTLE TOWARDS ME!
WE WERE REQUIRED TO DO THREE-QUARTER VIEWS--- MAIN STREET'S PASTEL PORTRAIT ARTISTS HAD THE LOCK ON PROFILES!
AS THE BOY HESITANTLY TURNED, I SAW THAT HIS RIGHT EYE WAS MISSING--- IT WAS JUST A HOLLOW SOCKET! A SINGLE STRAND OF FLESH CONNECTED HIS BROW TO THE TOP OF HIS CHEEK!

I COULD FEEL THE PRESENCE AND TENSION OF THE PARENTS BEHIND ME AS MY PENCIL APPROACHED THE BOARD!

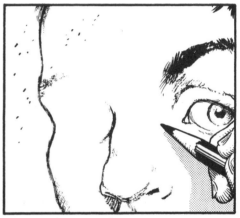

I DREW HIS LEFT EYE AND THEN THE REST OF HIS FACE! I SLOWLY SKETCHED, STALLING FOR TIME AS I TRIED TO GET A "READ" ON HIS PARENTS...

BY NOW THE TENSION WAS ALMOST *PALPABLE!* I COULDN'T DELAY ANY LONGER! I FINALLY WENT WITH MY GUT AND MADE A DECISION...

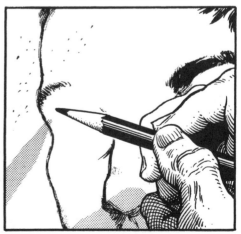

I TOOK A DEEP BREATH...
...AND I BEGAN TO DRAW...

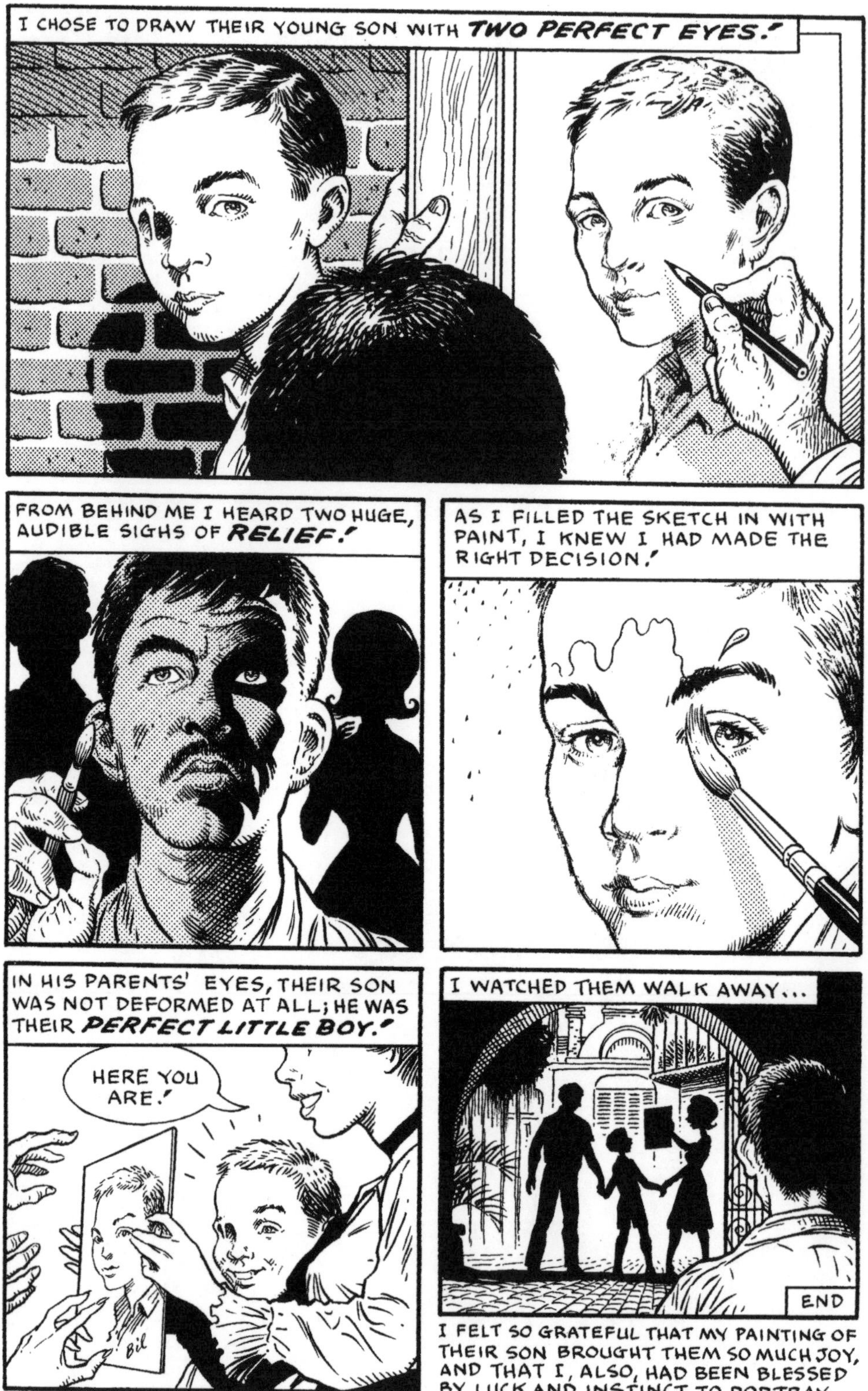
I CHOSE TO DRAW THEIR YOUNG SON WITH TWO PERFECT EYES!
FROM BEHIND ME I HEARD TWO HUGE, AUDIBLE SIGHS OF RELIEF!
AS I FILLED THE SKETCH IN WITH PAINT, I KNEW I HAD MADE THE RIGHT DECISION!
IN HIS PARENTS' EYES, THEIR SON WAS NOT DEFORMED AT ALL; HE WAS THEIR PERFECT LITTLE BOY!
HERE YOU ARE!
Bil
IT WAS JENNY THE CASHIER'S JOB TO PRESENT THE FINISHED PORTRAITS...
I WATCHED THEM WALK AWAY...
END
I FELT SO GRATEFUL THAT MY PAINTING OF THEIR SON BROUGHT THEM SO MUCH JOY, AND THAT I, ALSO, HAD BEEN BLESSED BY LUCK AND INSTINCT TO PORTRAY THAT SWEET BOY THROUGH THEIR EYES — THE EYES OF LOVE!!

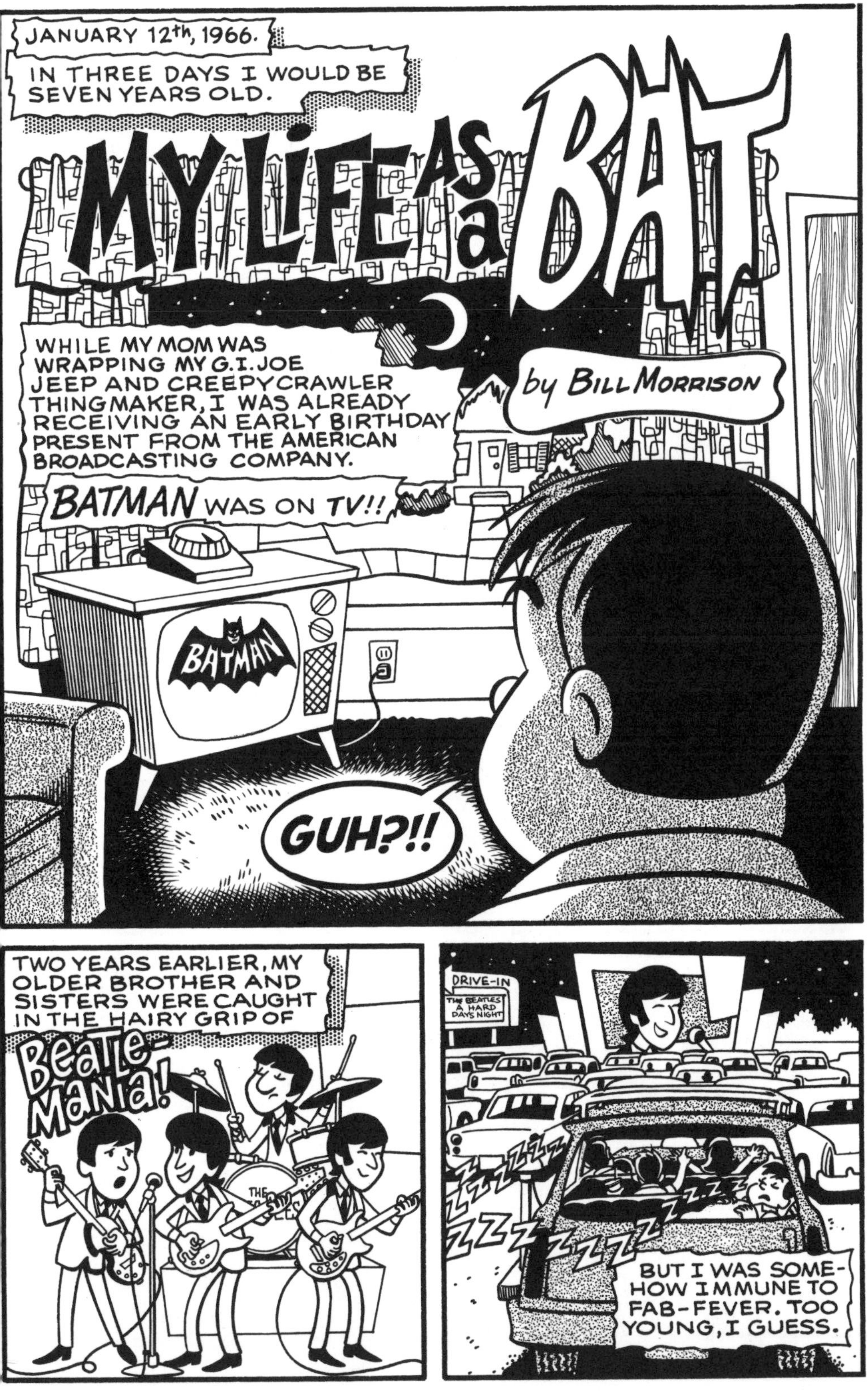

JANUARY 12th, 1966.
IN THREE DAYS I WOULD BE SEVEN YEARS OLD.
MY LIFE AS a BAT
by BILL MORRISON
WHILE MY MOM WAS WRAPPING MY G.I. JOE JEEP AND CREEPYCRAWLER THINGMAKER, I WAS ALREADY RECEIVING AN EARLY BIRTHDAY PRESENT FROM THE AMERICAN BROADCASTING COMPANY.
BATMAN WAS ON TV!!
BATMAN
GUH?!!
TWO YEARS EARLIER, MY OLDER BROTHER AND SISTERS WERE CAUGHT IN THE HAIRY GRIP OF
BEATLE-MANIA!
DRIVE-IN
THE BEATLES A HARD DAYS NIGHT
BUT I WAS SOME-HOW IMMUNE TO FAB-FEVER. TOO YOUNG, I GUESS.

41

FOREVER LASTED A LITTLE OVER TWENTY YEARS. IN 1989, TIM BURTON'S LONG-AWAITED BATMAN MOVIE OPENED AND BATMANIA INFECTED THE WORLD AGAIN.

AS AN ADULT, I FIGURED I'D BE IMMUNE TO IT THIS TIME AROUND, BUT NOPE.

IT DIDN'T HIT ME AS HARD AS IT HAD IN '66. I HAD THE T-SHIRTS, THE SNEAKERS, THE CEREAL WITH THE FREE BANK SHRINK-WRAPPED ON EVERY BOX...

HOW CAN THEY CALL THIS *"NEW"*? IT'S JUST CAPTAIN CRUNCH REFORMED INTO BAT SHAPES!

WELL, I HOPE YOU LIKE IT, BECAUSE YOU'VE GOT ELEVEN MORE BOXES TO FINISH!

(I STILL HAVE THOSE ELEVEN BOXES IN MY GARAGE, WAITING FOR EBAY.)

...BUT I WAS A GROWN MAN AND HAD NO DESIRE TO RUN AROUND DRESSED AS THE CAPED CRUSADER AGAIN. THAT IS, UNTIL...

AWESOME!

NOW YOU CAN OWN A Deluxe BATMAN COSTUME COMPLETE WITH UTILITY BUBBLE PIECES & SIX-PACK ONLY $300.00

IT WAS JUST LIKE THE COSTUME FROM THE MOVIE! 300 BONES WAS A LOT OF MONEY, BUT IT'D BE WORTH IT TO FINALLY HAVE THE BEST BATSUIT EVER!

HOW I IMAGINED I'D LOOK ➡

FOUR TO SIX WEEKS LATER, IT ARRIVED!

HOW I *ACTUALLY* LOOKED ➡

SO IT WASN'T THE BEST BATSUIT EVER...

...AT LEAST NOT AT FIRST. BUT A FEW YEARS LATER, THAT COSTUME WOULD HELP MAKE ME THE HERO I'D ALWAYS DREAMED OF BEING. I HAD CALLED MY SISTER TO TELL HER...

KAYRE AND I WILL BE BACK IN MICHIGAN AROUND HALLOWEEN.

GREAT!! YOU CAN HELP ME TAKE JUSTIN OUT TRICK-OR-TREATING. IT'S HIS FIRST TIME!

COOL! WHAT'S HE GOING AS?

I MADE HIM A *ROBIN* COSTUME!

NO WAY! ALICE, I'VE GOT A GREAT IDEA!

44

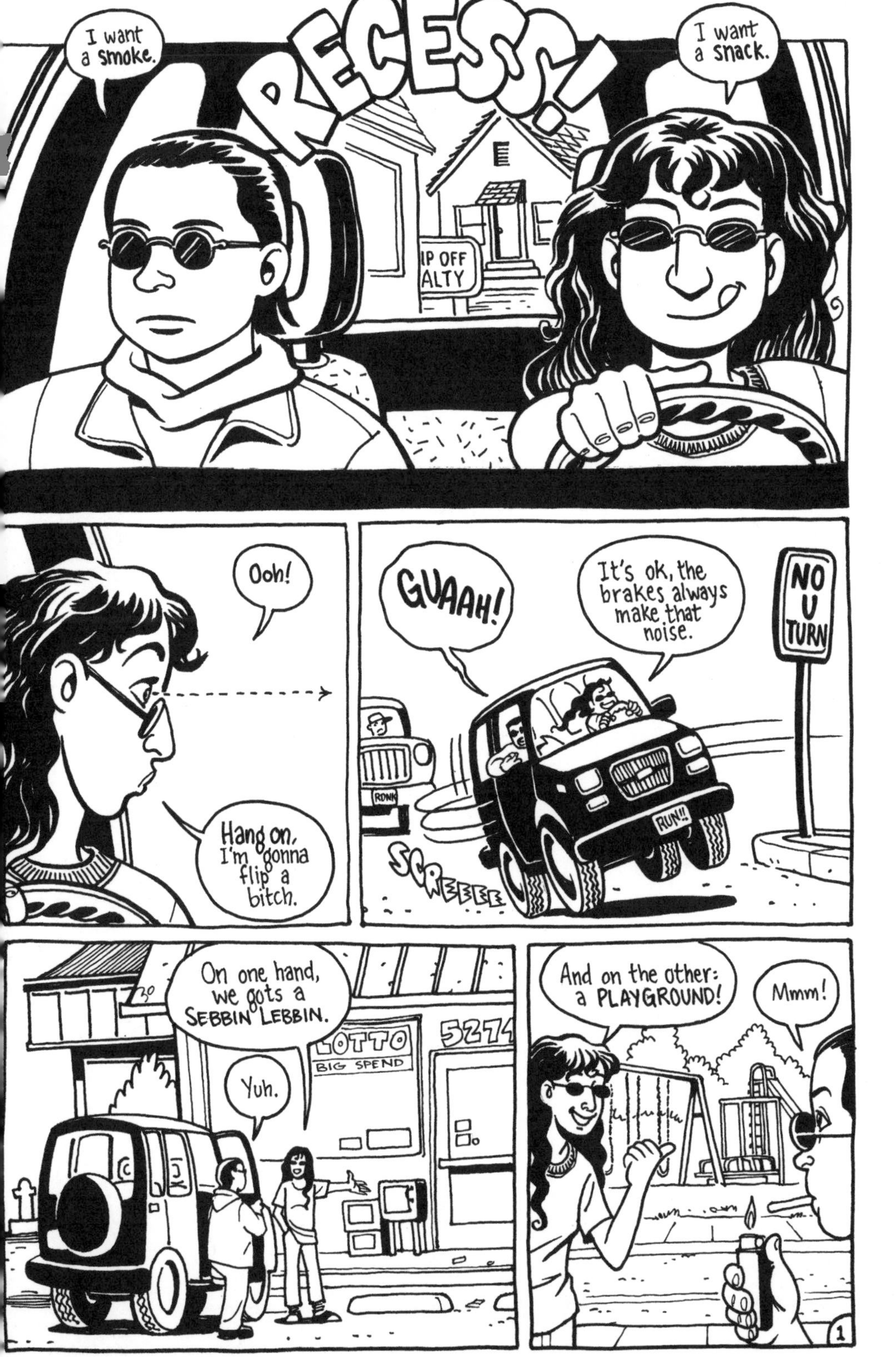

I want a smoke.
RECESS!
I want a snack.
IP OFF
ALTY
Ooh!
Hang on, I'm gonna flip a bitch.
GUAAH!
It's ok, the brakes always make that noise.
NO U TURN
RONK
RUN!!
SCREEEE
On one hand, we gots a SEBBIN LEBBIN.
LOTTO
BIG SPEND
5274
Yuh.
And on the other: a PLAYGROUND!
Mmm!

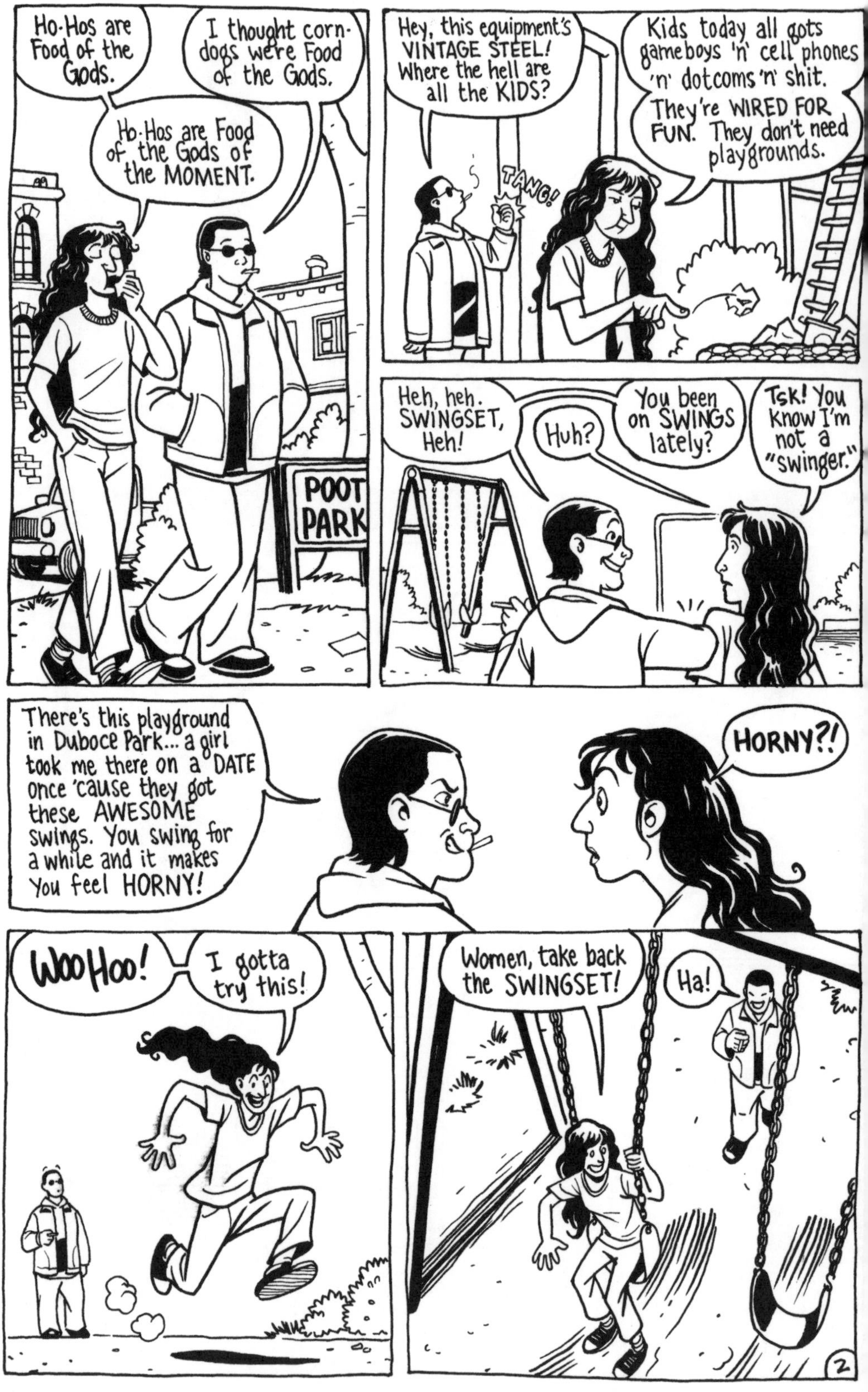

Ho·Hos are Food of the Gods.
I thought corn-dogs were Food of the Gods.
Ho·Hos are Food of the Gods of the MOMENT.
POOT PARK
Hey, this equipment's VINTAGE STEEL! Where the hell are all the KIDS?
TANG!
Kids today all gots gameboys 'n' cell phones 'n' dotcoms 'n' shit. They're WIRED FOR FUN. They don't need playgrounds.
Heh, heh. SWINGSET, Heh!
Huh?
You been on SWINGS lately?
Tsk! You know I'm not a "swinger."
There's this playground in Duboce Park... a girl took me there on a DATE once 'cause they got these AWESOME swings. You swing for a while and it makes you feel HORNY!
HORNY?!
WooHoo!
I gotta try this!
Women, take back the SWINGSET!
Ha!
2

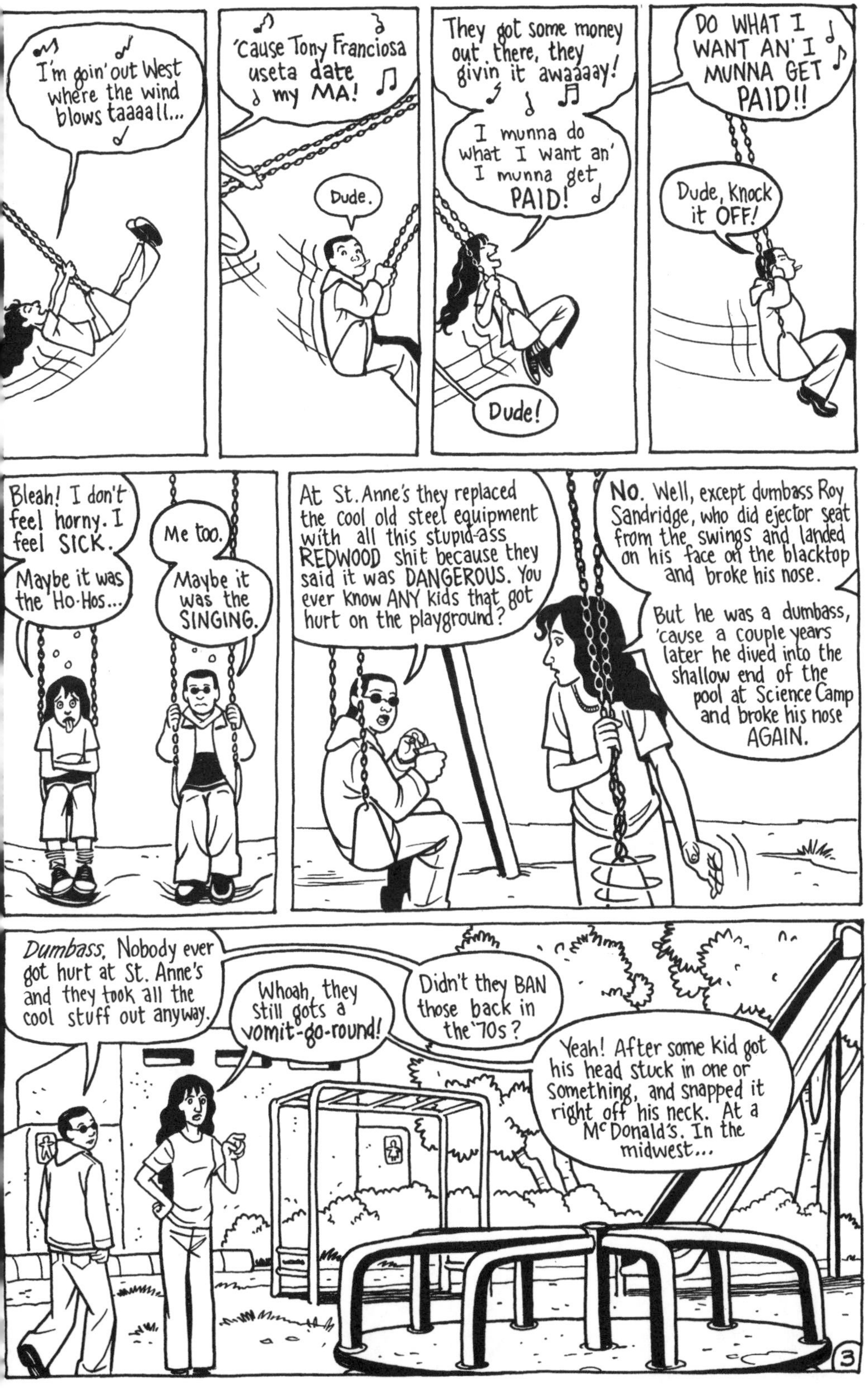

I'm goin' out West where the wind blows taaaall...
'Cause Tony Franciosa useta date my MA!
Dude.
They got some money out there, they givin it awaaaay!
I munna do what I want an' I munna get PAID!
Dude!
DO WHAT I WANT AN' I MUNNA GET PAID!!
Dude, Knock it OFF!
Bleah! I don't feel horny. I feel SICK.
Maybe it was the Ho-Hos...
Me too.
Maybe it was the SINGING.
At St. Anne's they replaced the cool old steel equipment with all this stupid-ass REDWOOD shit because they said it was DANGEROUS. You ever know ANY kids that got hurt on the playground?
No. Well, except dumbass Roy Sandridge, who did ejector seat from the swings and landed on his face on the blacktop and broke his nose.
But he was a dumbass, 'cause a couple years later he dived into the shallow end of the pool at Science Camp and broke his nose AGAIN.
Dumbass. Nobody ever got hurt at St. Anne's and they took all the cool stuff out anyway.
Whoah, they still gots a vomit-go-round!
Didn't they BAN those back in the '70s?
Yeah! After some kid got his head stuck in one or something, and snapped it right off his neck. At a McDonald's. In the midwest...
3

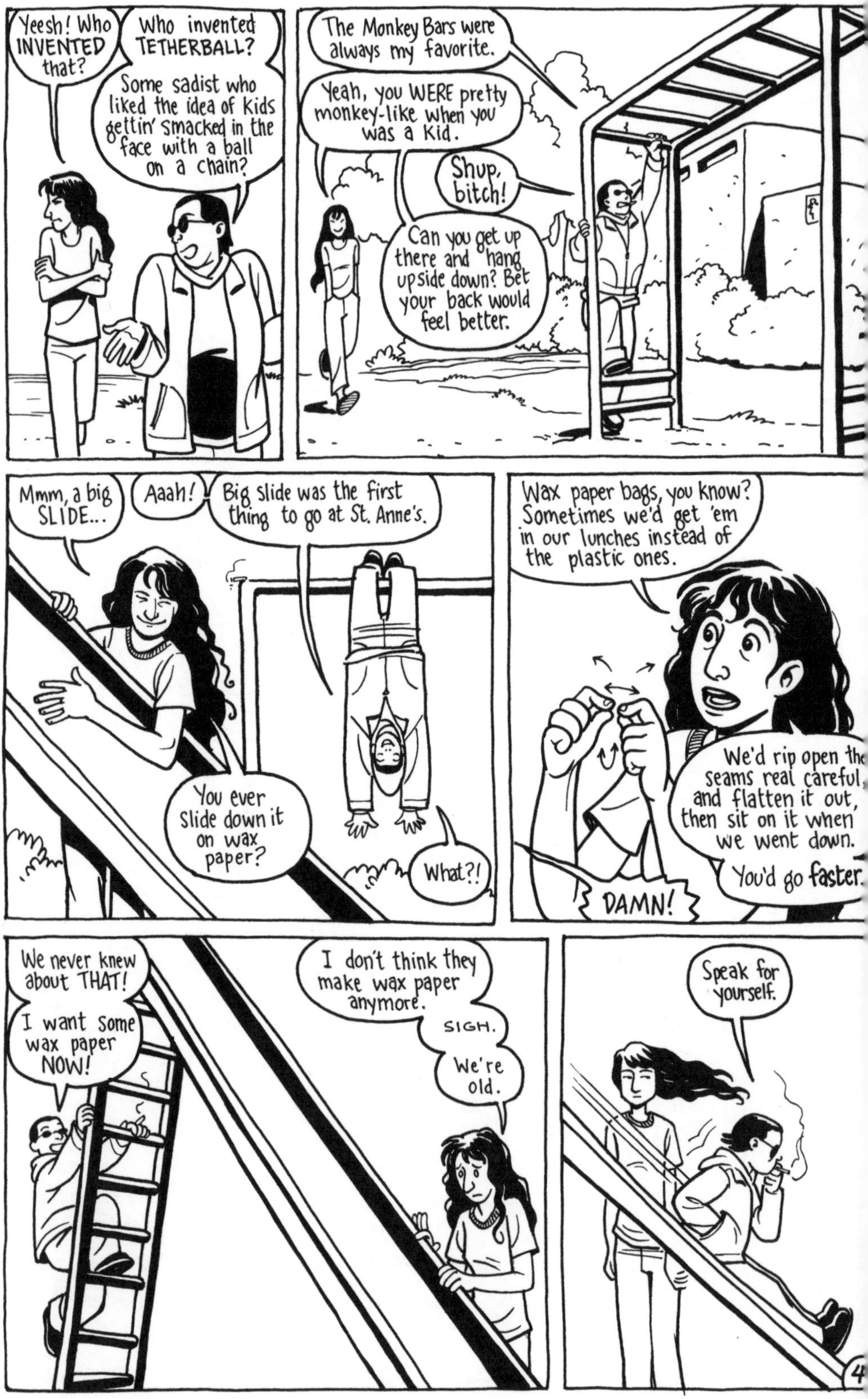

Yeesh! Who INVENTED that?
Who invented TETHERBALL?
Some sadist who liked the idea of kids gettin' smacked in the face with a ball on a chain?
The Monkey Bars were always my favorite.
Yeah, you WERE pretty monkey-like when you was a kid.
Shup, bitch!
Can you get up there and hang upside down? Bet your back would feel better.
Mmm, a big SLIDE...
Aaah!
Big slide was the first thing to go at St. Anne's.
You ever slide down it on wax paper?
What?!
Wax paper bags, you know? Sometimes we'd get 'em in our lunches instead of the plastic ones.
We'd rip open the seams real careful, and flatten it out, then sit on it when we went down.
You'd go faster.
DAMN!
We never knew about THAT!
I want some wax paper NOW!
I don't think they make wax paper anymore.
SIGH.
We're old.
Speak for yourself.

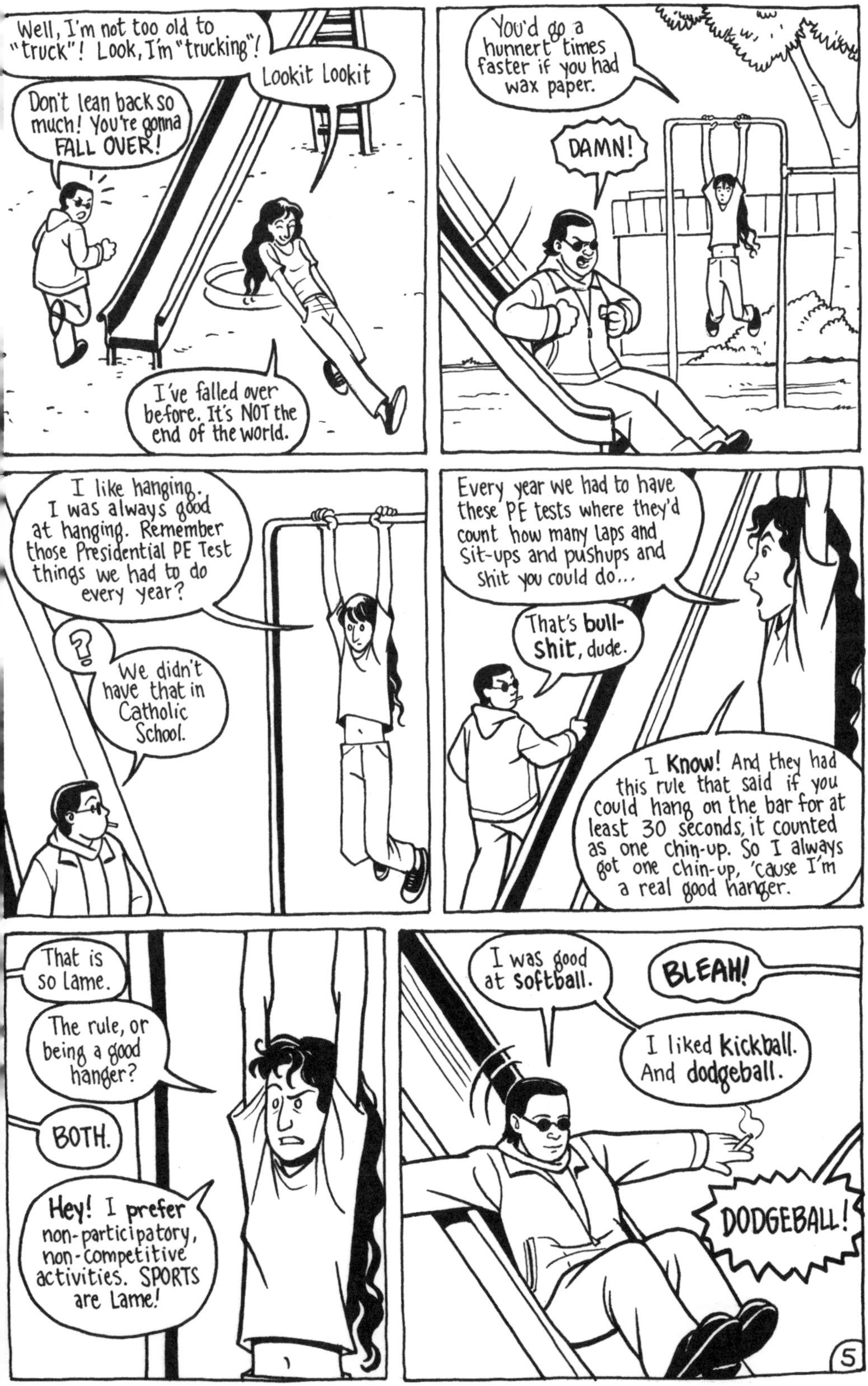
Well, I'm not too old to "truck"! Look, I'm "trucking"!
Lookit Lookit
Don't lean back so much! You're gonna FALL OVER!
I've falled over before. It's NOT the end of the world.
You'd go a hunnert times faster if you had wax paper.
DAMN!
I like hanging. I was always good at hanging. Remember those Presidential PE Test things we had to do every year?
?
We didn't have that in Catholic School.
Every year we had to have these PE tests where they'd count how many laps and sit-ups and pushups and shit you could do...
That's bull-shit, dude.
I Know! And they had this rule that said if you could hang on the bar for at least 30 seconds, it counted as one chin-up. So I always got one chin-up, 'cause I'm a real good hanger.
That is so Lame.
The rule, or being a good hanger?
BOTH.
Hey! I prefer non-participatory, non-competitive activities. SPORTS are Lame!
I was good at softball.
BLEAH!
I liked kickball. And dodgeball.
DODGEBALL!
5

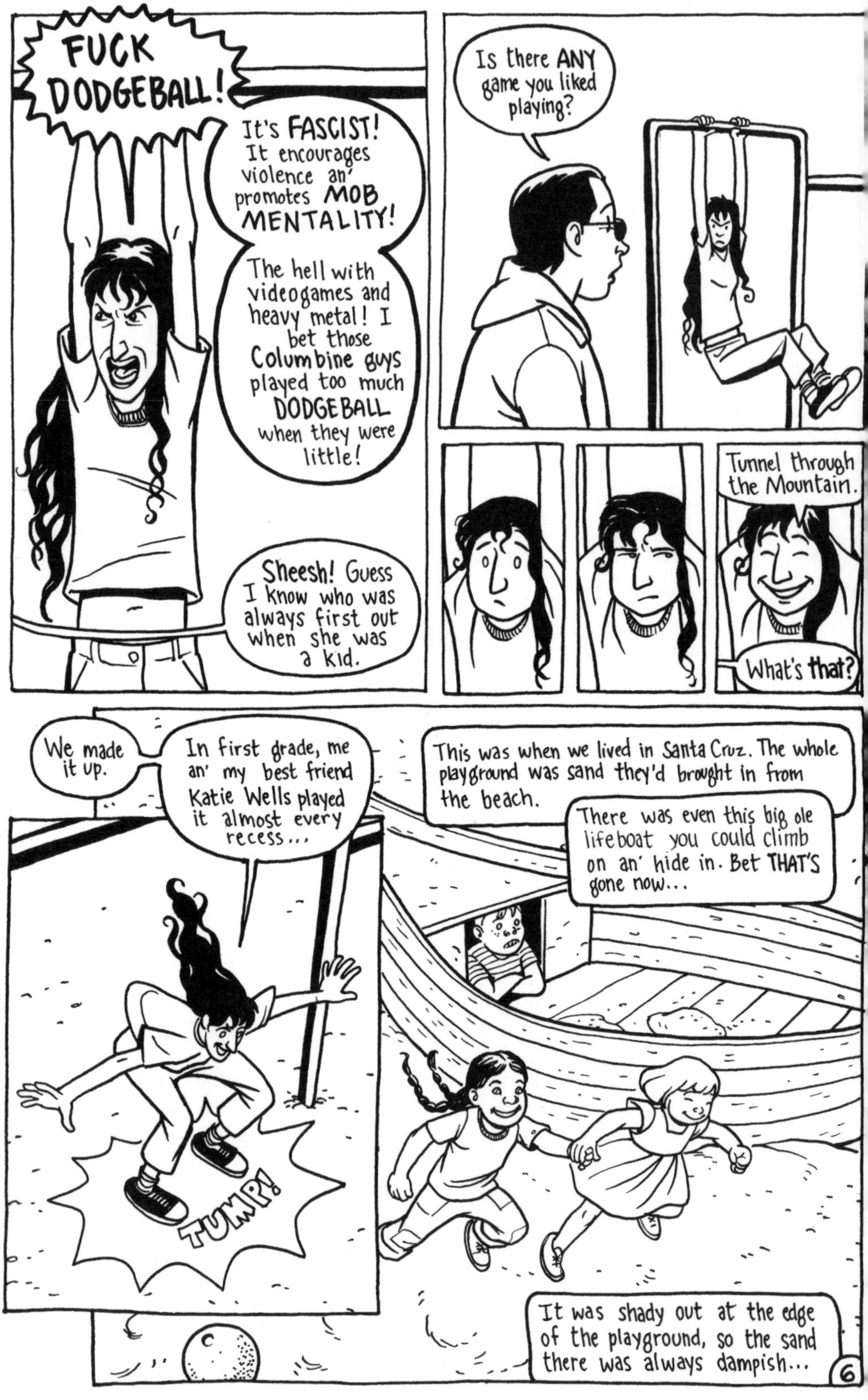
FUCK DODGEBALL!
It's FASCIST! It encourages violence an' promotes MOB MENTALITY!
The hell with videogames and heavy metal! I bet those Columbine guys played too much DODGEBALL when they were little!
Sheesh! Guess I know who was always first out when she was a kid.
Is there ANY game you liked playing?
Tunnel through the Mountain.
What's that?
We made it up.
In first grade, me an' my best friend Katie Wells played it almost every recess...
This was when we lived in Santa Cruz. The whole playground was sand they'd brought in from the beach.
There was even this big ole lifeboat you could climb on an' hide in. Bet THAT'S gone now...
TUMP!
It was shady out at the edge of the playground, so the sand there was always dampish...
6

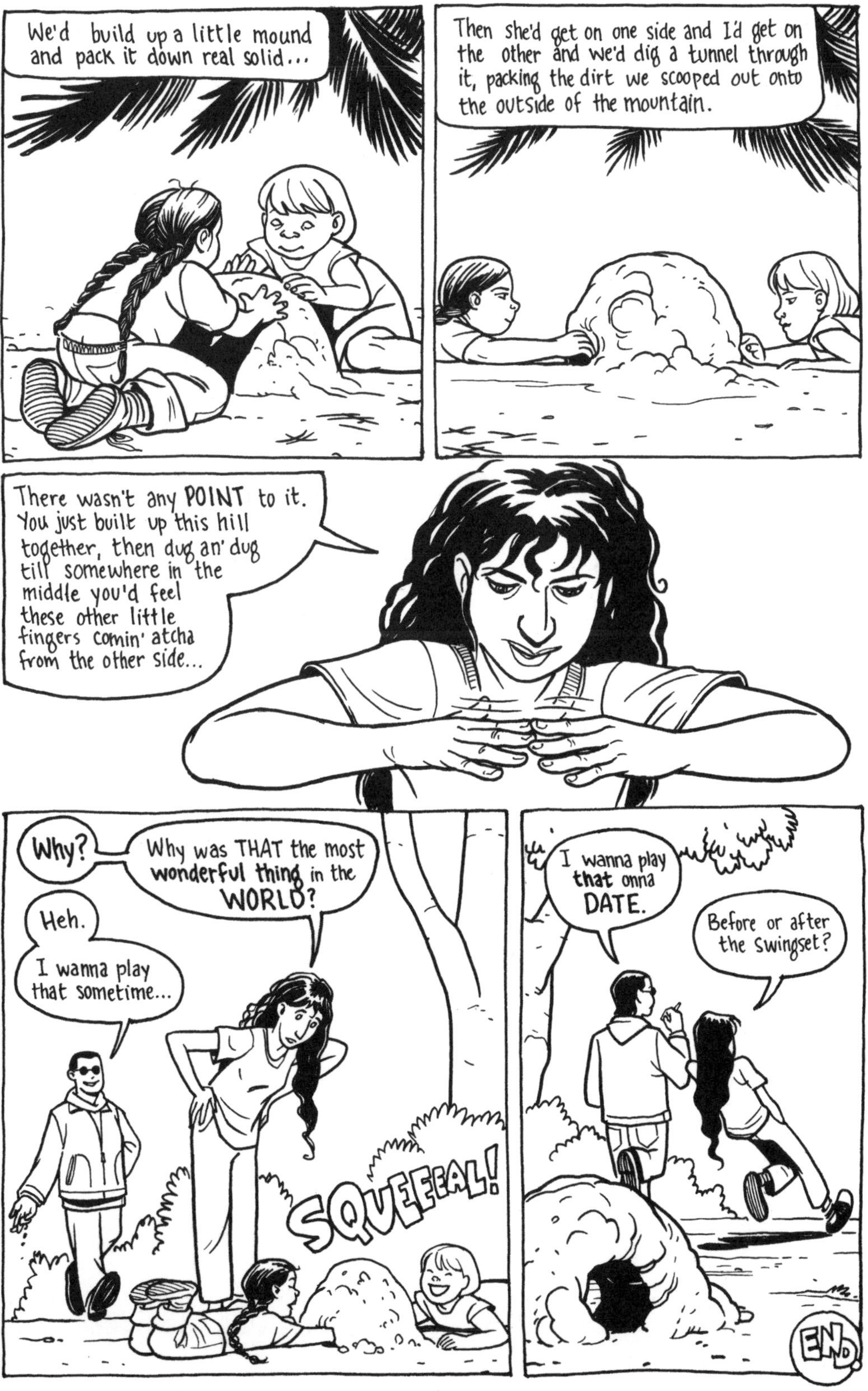
We'd build up a little mound and pack it down real solid...
Then she'd get on one side and I'd get on the other and we'd dig a tunnel through it, packing the dirt we scooped out onto the outside of the mountain.
There wasn't any POINT to it. You just built up this hill together, then dug an' dug till somewhere in the middle you'd feel these other little fingers comin' atcha from the other side...
Why?
Why was THAT the most wonderful thing in the WORLD?
Heh.
I wanna play that sometime...
SQUEEEAL!
I wanna play that onna DATE.
Before or after the swingset?
END

52

Coda

I have lost my sense of humour.

aw, the poor bloke. Somebody help him up.

It's funny.

Throwing trash on the footpath isn't funny. Somebody might hurt himself. It could be me.

Now, that would be truly hilarious.

Here's another example: boy's party invitation.

what shall I bring?

I am given to thinking that boys acquired nice manners and considerateness since I last paid attention, but then the twist:

Aaron said he'll bring the fart-gas.

There was a time when I would have easily built a whole page of comic dialogue around such a situation.

I try to run all the setup variations through my noodle.

who's bringing the honey-puffs?

you just bring yourself.

But it ain't happening, nothin's doing.

GET YER GUN

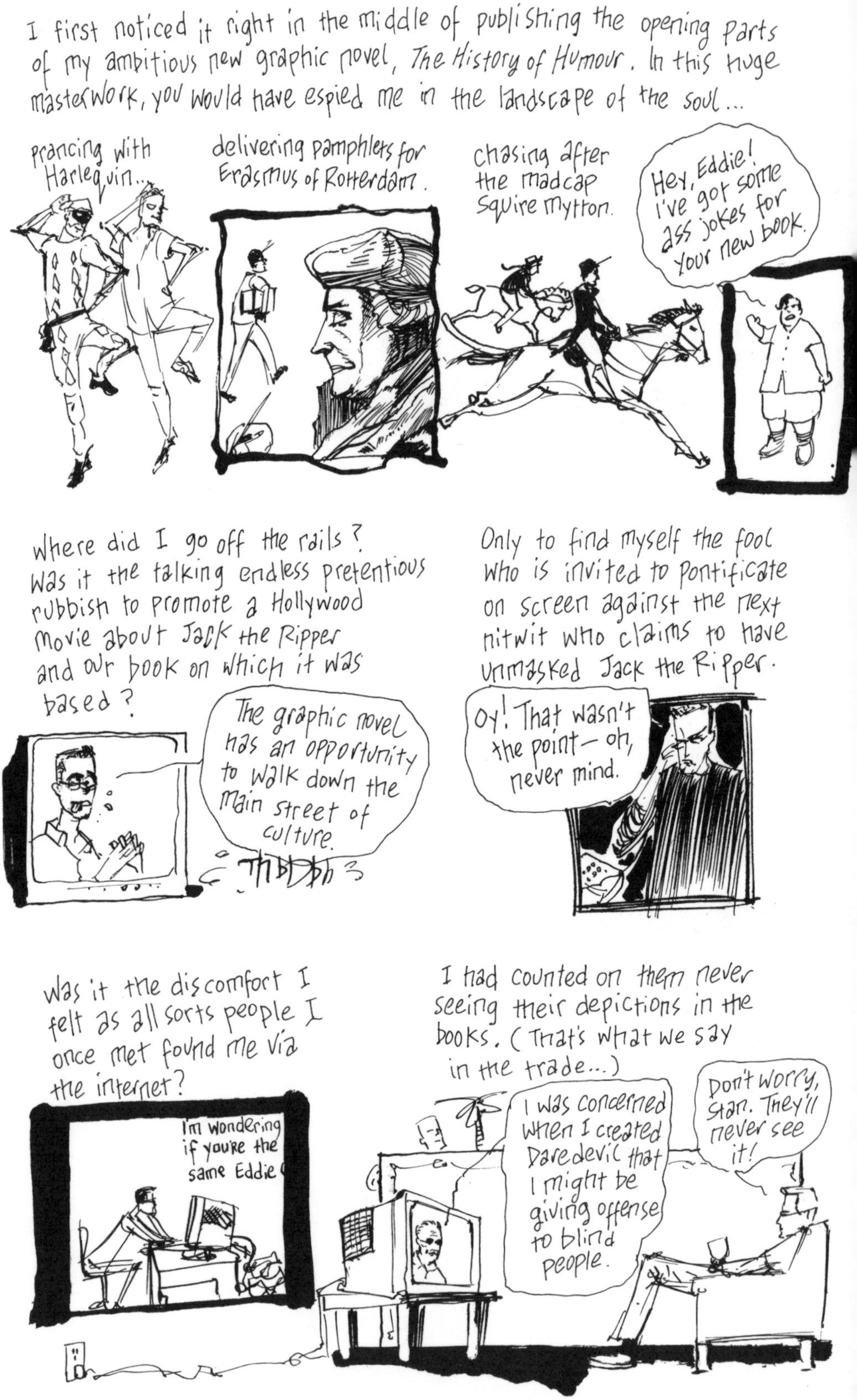
I first noticed it right in the middle of publishing the opening parts of my ambitious new graphic novel, The History of Humour. In this huge masterwork, you would have espied me in the landscape of the soul...
prancing with Harlequin...
delivering pamphlets for Erasmus of Rotterdam.
chasing after the madcap Squire Mytton.
Hey, Eddie! I've got some ass jokes for your new book.
Where did I go off the rails? Was it the talking endless pretentious rubbish to promote a Hollywood movie about Jack the Ripper and our book on which it was based?
The graphic novel has an opportunity to walk down the main street of culture.
Only to find myself the fool who is invited to pontificate on screen against the next nitwit who claims to have unmasked Jack the Ripper.
Oy! That wasn't the point— oh, never mind.
Was it the discomfort I felt as all sorts people I once met found me via the internet?
I'm wondering if you're the same Eddie
I had counted on them never seeing their depictions in the books. (That's what we say in the trade...)
I was concerned when I created Daredevil that I might be giving offense to blind people.
Don't worry, Stan. They'll never see it!

Was it the strange, mystifying ailments I have started to develop? I should have recognized them as symptoms of the loss of a sense of humour.

The tag-team specialists:

Was it the increasingly complex technology that sapped my energy?

Perhaps it was my book-store distributor going kerplunk, owing me fifty thousand bucks.

Or was it just the whole undignified rot that is comic books? Our fraternity complains when the media treats the whole subject as gaudy, puerile foolishness ...but we give the awards to Batman just the same.

I vow that I will never again use the term "graphic novel" or argue that comics are art.

Then, like Pacino in Godfather II, I set about eliminating my enemies one by one.

First, I contrive to fall out with anyone who is still working with me.

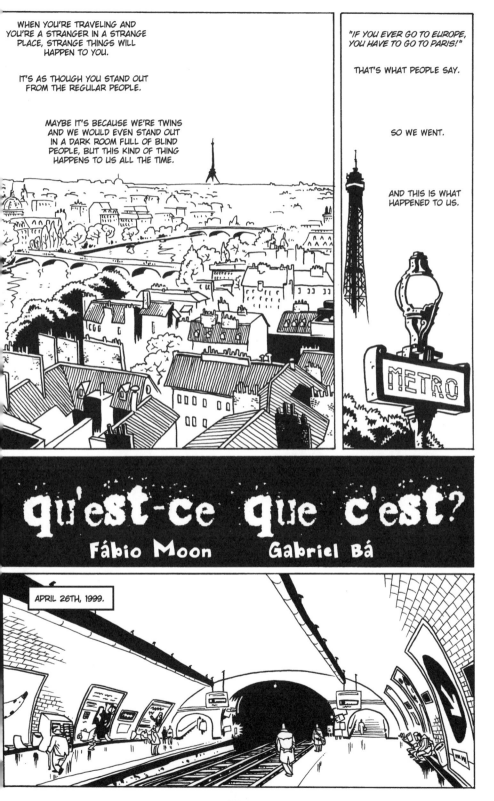

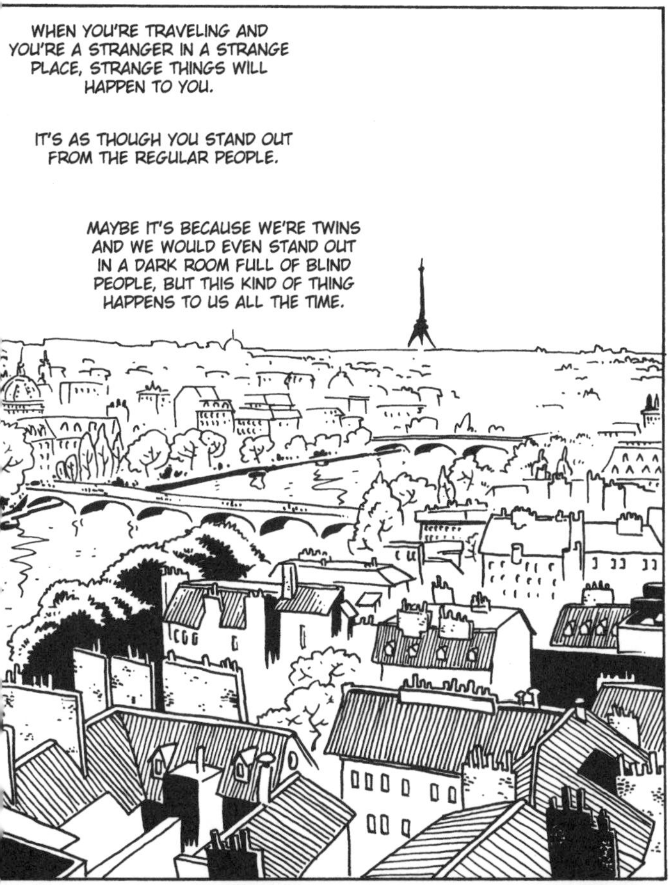
WHEN YOU'RE TRAVELING AND YOU'RE A STRANGER IN A STRANGE PLACE, STRANGE THINGS WILL HAPPEN TO YOU.
IT'S AS THOUGH YOU STAND OUT FROM THE REGULAR PEOPLE.
MAYBE IT'S BECAUSE WE'RE TWINS AND WE WOULD EVEN STAND OUT IN A DARK ROOM FULL OF BLIND PEOPLE, BUT THIS KIND OF THING HAPPENS TO US ALL THE TIME.

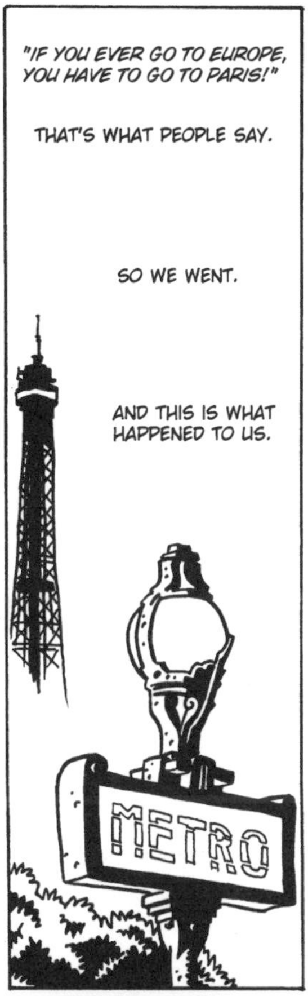
"IF YOU EVER GO TO EUROPE, YOU HAVE TO GO TO PARIS!"
THAT'S WHAT PEOPLE SAY.
SO WE WENT.
AND THIS IS WHAT HAPPENED TO US.
METRO

qu'est-ce que c'est?

Fábio Moon Gabriel Bá

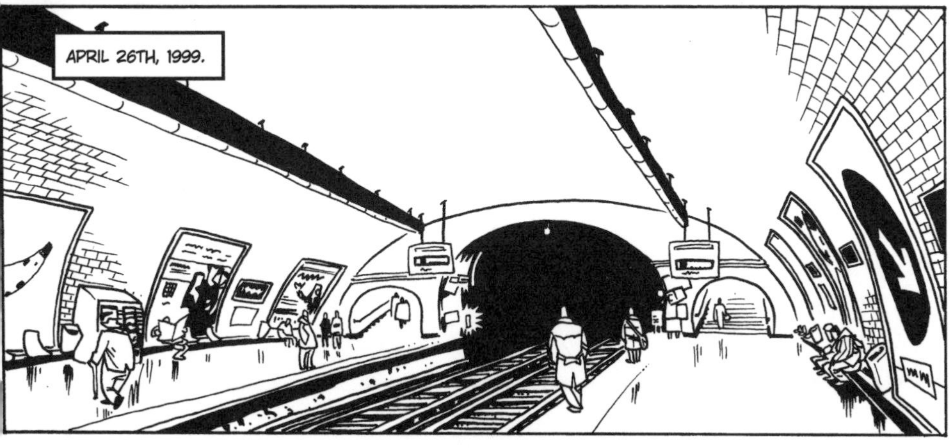
APRIL 26TH, 1999.

69

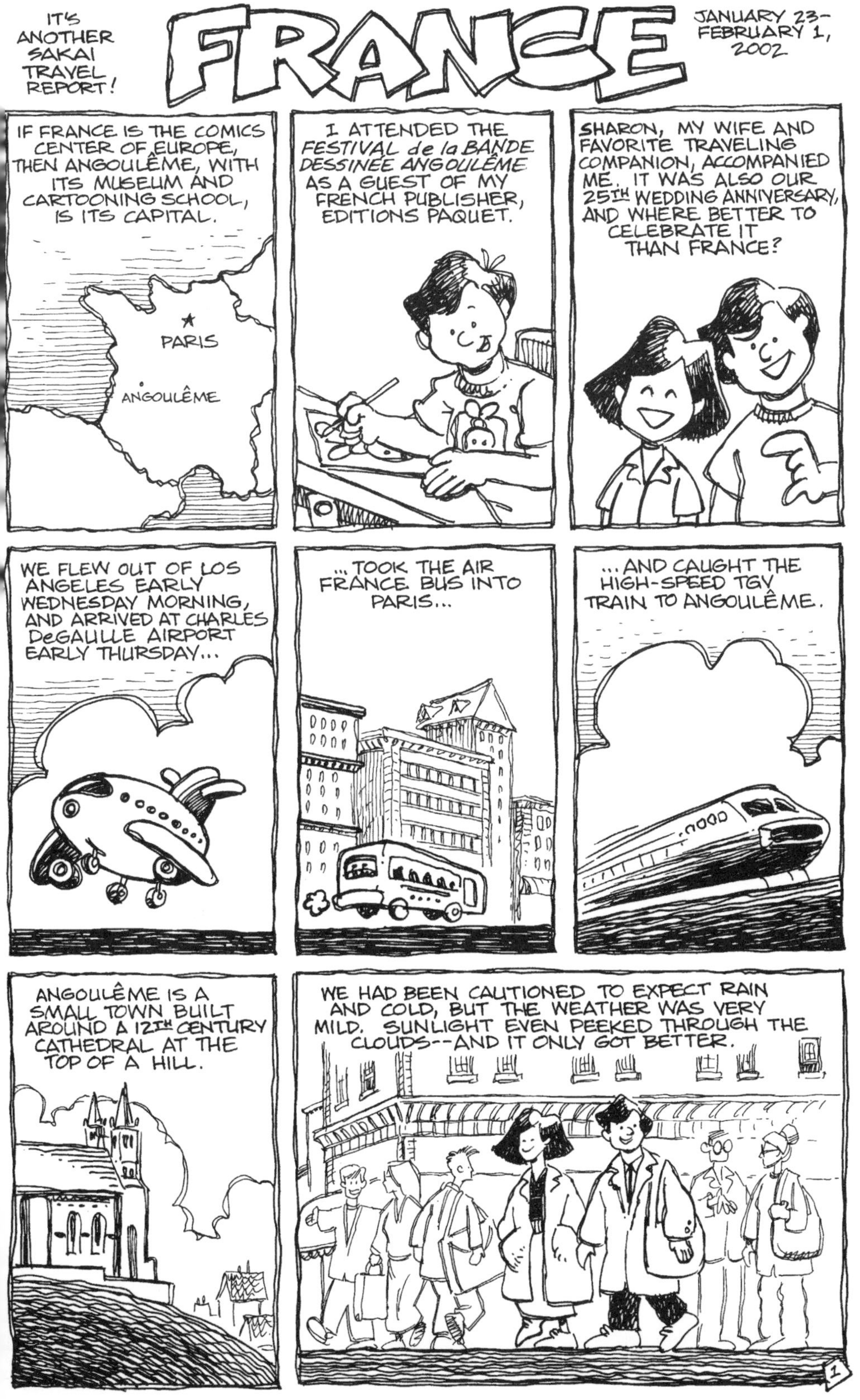

IT'S ANOTHER SAKAI TRAVEL REPORT!
FRANCE
JANUARY 23–FEBRUARY 1, 2002
IF FRANCE IS THE COMICS CENTER OF EUROPE, THEN ANGOULÊME, WITH ITS MUSEUM AND CARTOONING SCHOOL, IS ITS CAPITAL.
PARIS
ANGOULÊME
I ATTENDED THE FESTIVAL de la BANDE DESSINÉE ANGOULÊME AS A GUEST OF MY FRENCH PUBLISHER, EDITIONS PAQUET.
SHARON, MY WIFE AND FAVORITE TRAVELING COMPANION, ACCOMPANIED ME. IT WAS ALSO OUR 25TH WEDDING ANNIVERSARY, AND WHERE BETTER TO CELEBRATE IT THAN FRANCE?
WE FLEW OUT OF LOS ANGELES EARLY WEDNESDAY MORNING, AND ARRIVED AT CHARLES DeGAULLE AIRPORT EARLY THURSDAY...
...TOOK THE AIR FRANCE BUS INTO PARIS...
...AND CAUGHT THE HIGH-SPEED TGV TRAIN TO ANGOULÊME.
ANGOULÊME IS A SMALL TOWN BUILT AROUND A 12TH CENTURY CATHEDRAL AT THE TOP OF A HILL.
WE HAD BEEN CAUTIONED TO EXPECT RAIN AND COLD, BUT THE WEATHER WAS VERY MILD. SUNLIGHT EVEN PEEKED THROUGH THE CLOUDS--AND IT ONLY GOT BETTER.
1

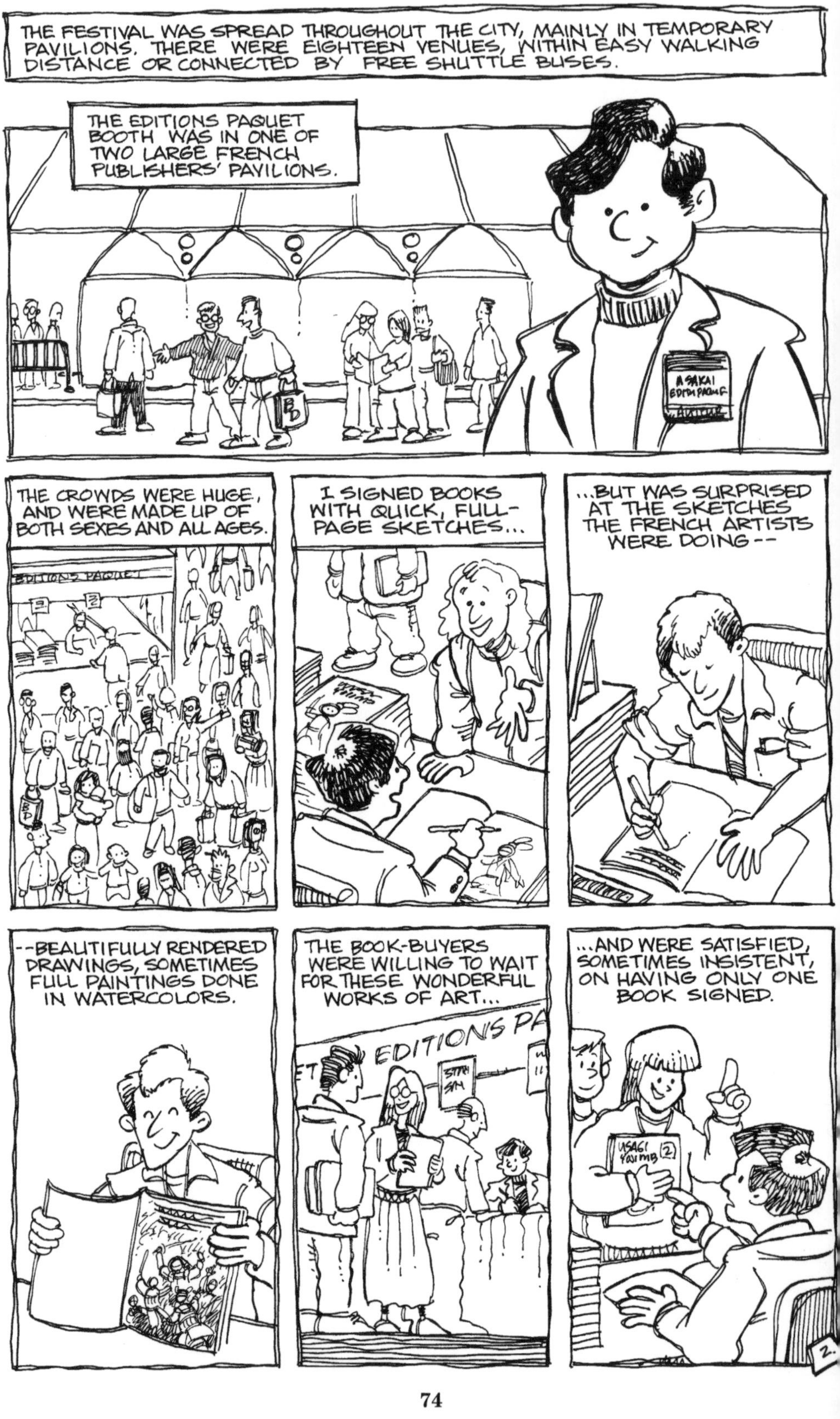
THE FESTIVAL WAS SPREAD THROUGHOUT THE CITY, MAINLY IN TEMPORARY PAVILIONS. THERE WERE EIGHTEEN VENUES, WITHIN EASY WALKING DISTANCE OR CONNECTED BY FREE SHUTTLE BUSES.
THE EDITIONS PAQUET BOOTH WAS IN ONE OF TWO LARGE FRENCH PUBLISHERS' PAVILIONS.
THE CROWDS WERE HUGE, AND WERE MADE UP OF BOTH SEXES AND ALL AGES.
I SIGNED BOOKS WITH QUICK, FULL-PAGE SKETCHES...
...BUT WAS SURPRISED AT THE SKETCHES THE FRENCH ARTISTS WERE DOING--
--BEAUTIFULLY RENDERED DRAWINGS, SOMETIMES FULL PAINTINGS DONE IN WATERCOLORS.
THE BOOK-BUYERS WERE WILLING TO WAIT FOR THESE WONDERFUL WORKS OF ART...
...AND WERE SATISFIED, SOMETIMES INSISTENT, ON HAVING ONLY ONE BOOK SIGNED.

I WAS TOLD THAT ATTENDANCE AT THE FESTIVAL WAS ABOUT 250,000.

AS I SAID, ANGOULÊME IS A FAIRLY SMALL TOWN, SO WE STAYED IN COGNAC, ABOUT 40 km. AWAY.

COGNAC IS CLOSER TO THE COAST, AND THE SEAFOOD WAS OUTSTANDING.

ONE NIGHT, I ATE STINGRAY.

ANOTHER SUPPER WAS *FRUITS de la MARE* -- A SEAFOOD FEAST THAT WAS NOT TO BE BELIEVED.

AND I DISCOVERED THE JOYS OF REAL CREME BRULEE.

YUMMY.

WE ALSO HAD A CHANCE TO TOUR THE SIGHTS OF ANGOULÊME, INCLUDING ITS WORLD-FAMOUS CARTOON MUSEUM. ON THE GROUND OUTSIDE THE MUSEUM ARE CEMENT SQUARES WITH DRAWINGS AND SIGNATURES OF FAMOUS CARTOONISTS. IT WAS A CARTOONIST VERSION OF HOLLYWOOD'S MANN'S CHINESE THEATRE.

LOOK-- THERE'S WILL EISNER.

1999

THERE WAS AN EXHIBITION OF AMERICAN INDEPENDENT COMICS, OF WHICH MY USAGI YOJIMBO WAS A PART.

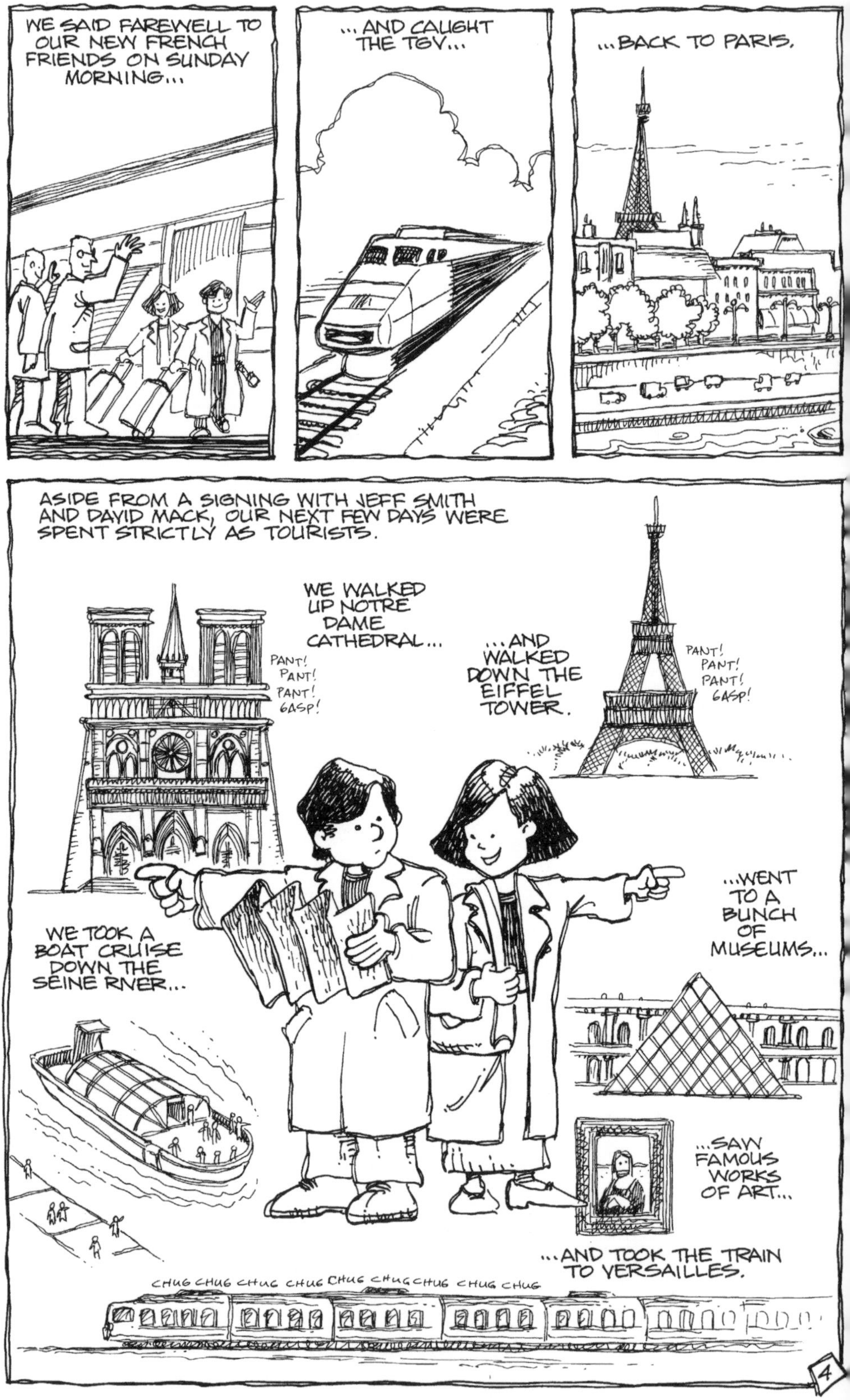
WE SAID FAREWELL TO OUR NEW FRENCH FRIENDS ON SUNDAY MORNING...
...AND CAUGHT THE TGV...
...BACK TO PARIS.
ASIDE FROM A SIGNING WITH JEFF SMITH AND DAVID MACK, OUR NEXT FEW DAYS WERE SPENT STRICTLY AS TOURISTS.
WE WALKED UP NOTRE DAME CATHEDRAL...
PANT! PANT! PANT! GASP!
...AND WALKED DOWN THE EIFFEL TOWER.
PANT! PANT! PANT! GASP!
WE TOOK A BOAT CRUISE DOWN THE SEINE RIVER...
...WENT TO A BUNCH OF MUSEUMS...
...SAW FAMOUS WORKS OF ART...
...AND TOOK THE TRAIN TO VERSAILLES.
CHUG CHUG CHUG CHUG CHUG CHUG CHUG CHUG CHUG
4

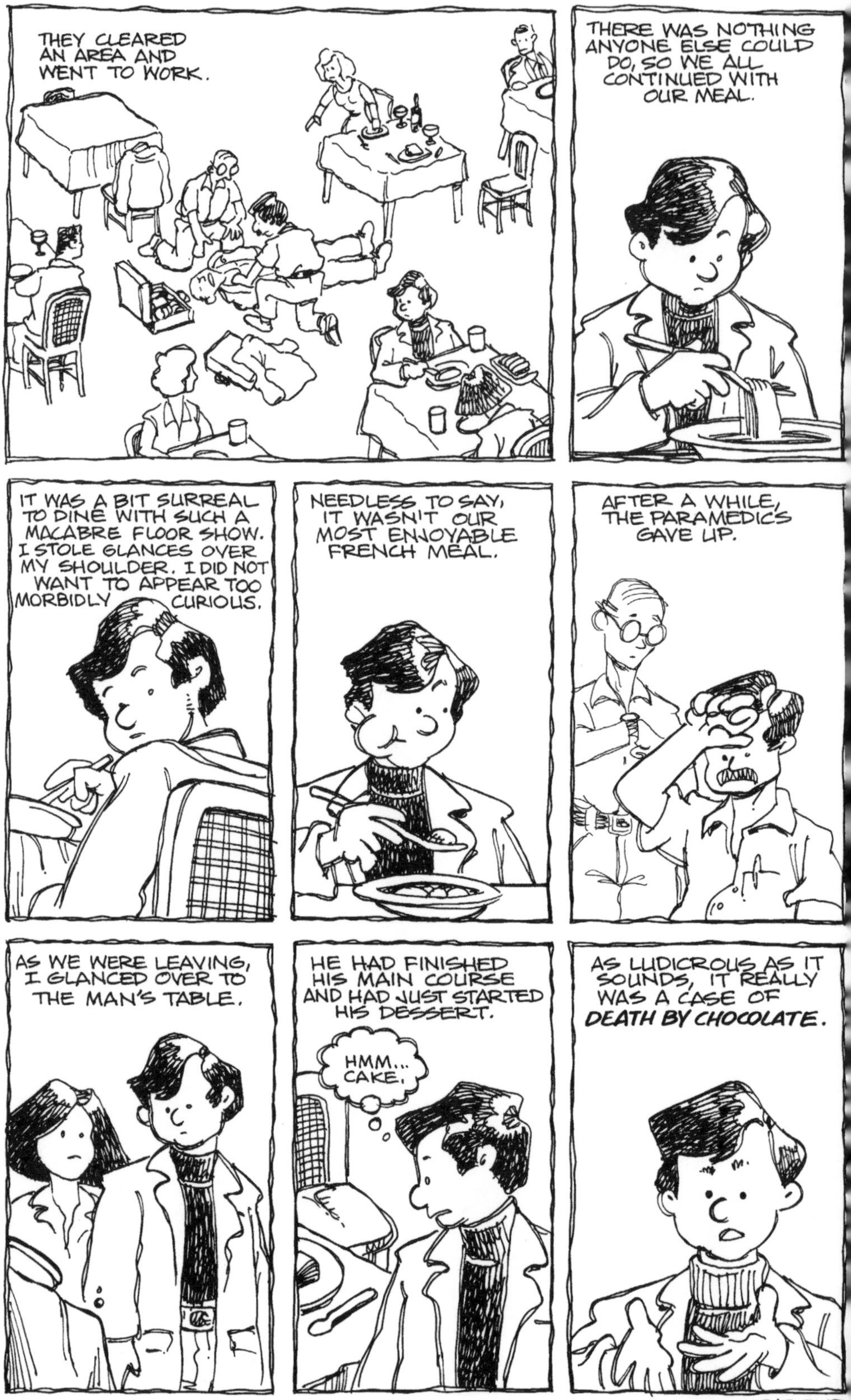
THEY CLEARED AN AREA AND WENT TO WORK.
THERE WAS NOTHING ANYONE ELSE COULD DO, SO WE ALL CONTINUED WITH OUR MEAL.
IT WAS A BIT SURREAL TO DINE WITH SUCH A MACABRE FLOOR SHOW. I STOLE GLANCES OVER MY SHOULDER. I DID NOT WANT TO APPEAR TOO MORBIDLY CURIOUS.
NEEDLESS TO SAY, IT WASN'T OUR MOST ENJOYABLE FRENCH MEAL.
AFTER A WHILE, THE PARAMEDICS GAVE UP.
AS WE WERE LEAVING, I GLANCED OVER TO THE MAN'S TABLE.
HE HAD FINISHED HIS MAIN COURSE AND HAD JUST STARTED HIS DESSERT.
HMM... CAKE.
AS LUDICROUS AS IT SOUNDS, IT REALLY WAS A CASE OF DEATH BY CHOCOLATE.
THE END.

MEMORY IS ANOTHER COUNTRY, JOURNEYS' BORDERS BLEND, BEGINNINGS BECOME ENDS.

THE CAFÉ OWNER'S COMPASSION HAD APPARENTLY RUN DRY AFTER YESTERDAY'S MATINEE.

SAID HE'D SEEN IT ALL BEFORE.

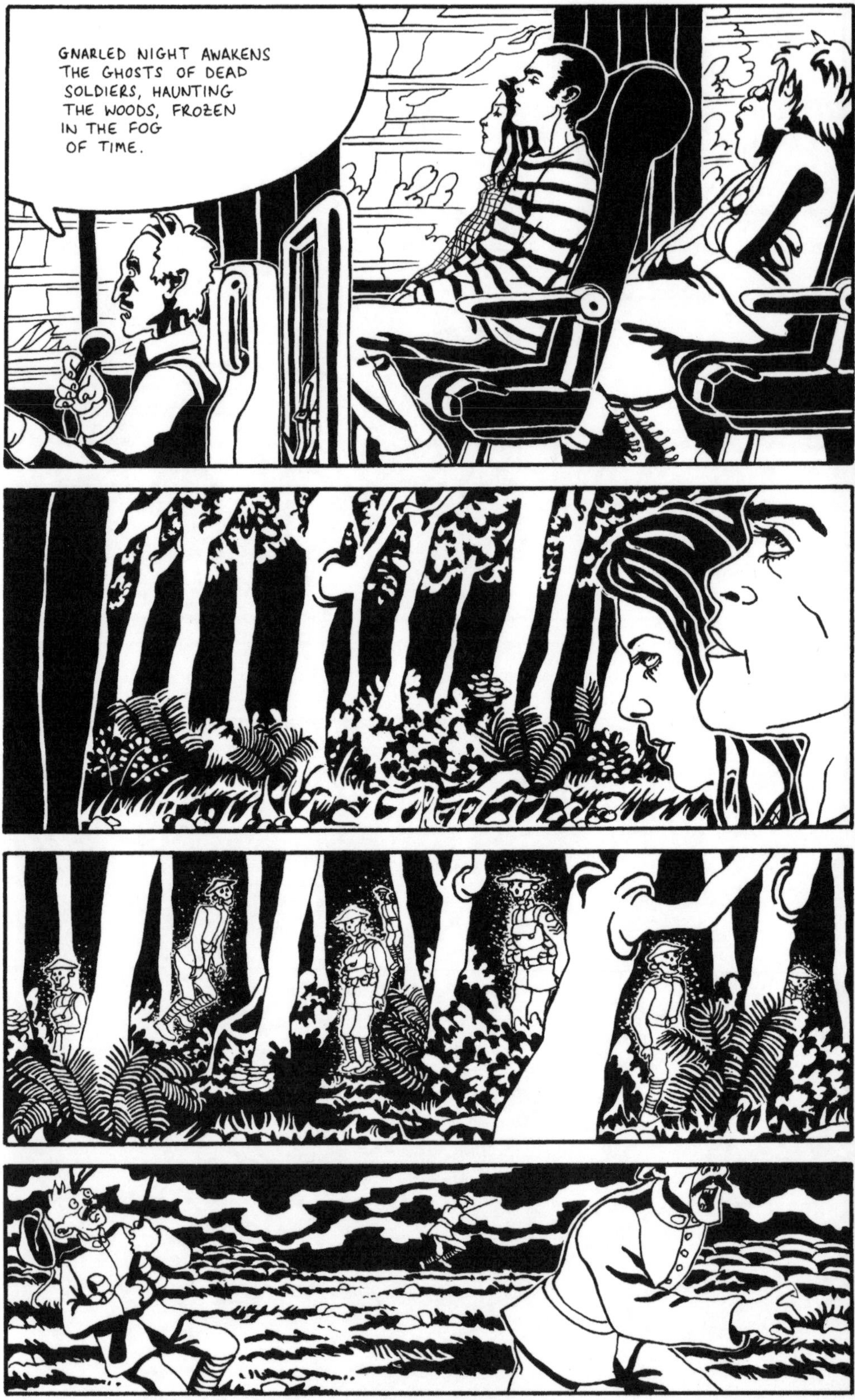
GNARLED NIGHT AWAKENS THE GHOSTS OF DEAD SOLDIERS, HAUNTING THE WOODS, FROZEN IN THE FOG OF TIME.

AS IT TURNED OUT, THERE WAS NO SEARCH, BUT THE OPAQUE INNER WORKINGS OF CUSTOMS AND IMMIGRATION CONTROL BECAME GROTESQUELY TRANSPARENT.

A PATINA OF GREASE AND CIGARETTE ASH COVERED THE EARLY MORNING BUS STATION.

TRAVELLING TRANSIENTS HALF ASLEEP ON HALF-STRENGTH COFFEE, POORLY FUEL FOR A THREE-COACH JOURNEY.

YOU DISGUST ME!

PEOPLE LIKE YOU MAKE ME SICK!

A BUSY VOICE WITH GREY SHOES REFUSED TO LET US ON THE BUS.

BUT WE RESERVED SEATS LAST WEEK...

WE WERE STRANDED IN TIMETABLE LIMBO.

THE PROS AND CONS OF THE ECONOMAN'S EUROPE.

A CURTAIN OF THIN SUSPENDED DRIZZLE BLURRED THE BORDER, THE HALF-EMPTY BUS DRIFTED INTO A CLOUD, WE WERE ALMOST HOME.

84

One of the parishioners, an elderly woman named Lily, became my friend.

I tended the lawns and trees while Lily looked after the flowers.

She had always lived in the parish. Her parents were buried in that cemetery.

I often saw her put flowers on their graves.

FATHER

MOTHER

One day Lily pulled me aside...

Will you plant a tree for me today?

Sure, I'll be happy to do it.

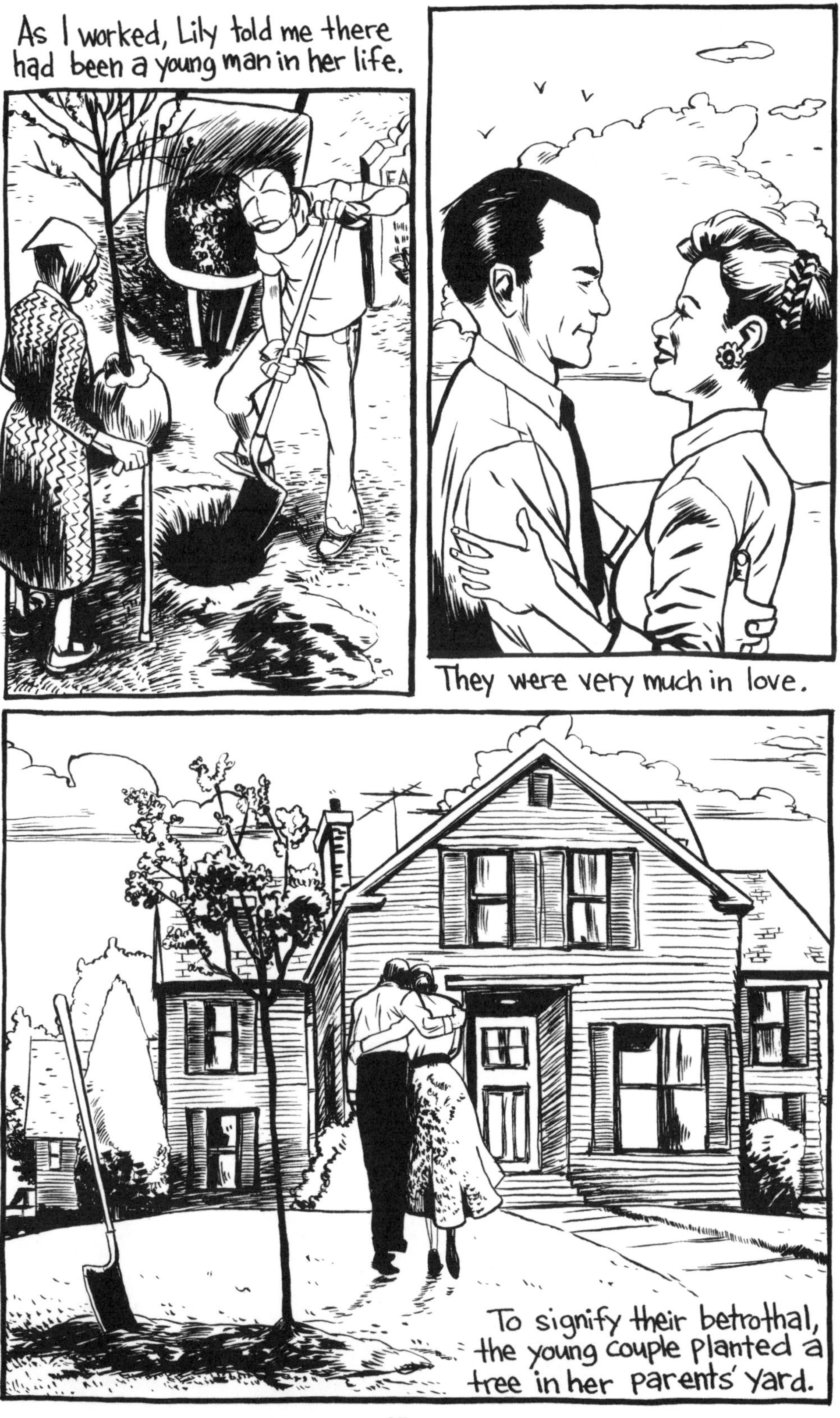
As I worked, Lily told me there had been a young man in her life.
They were very much in love.
To signify their betrothal, the young couple planted a tree in her parents' yard.

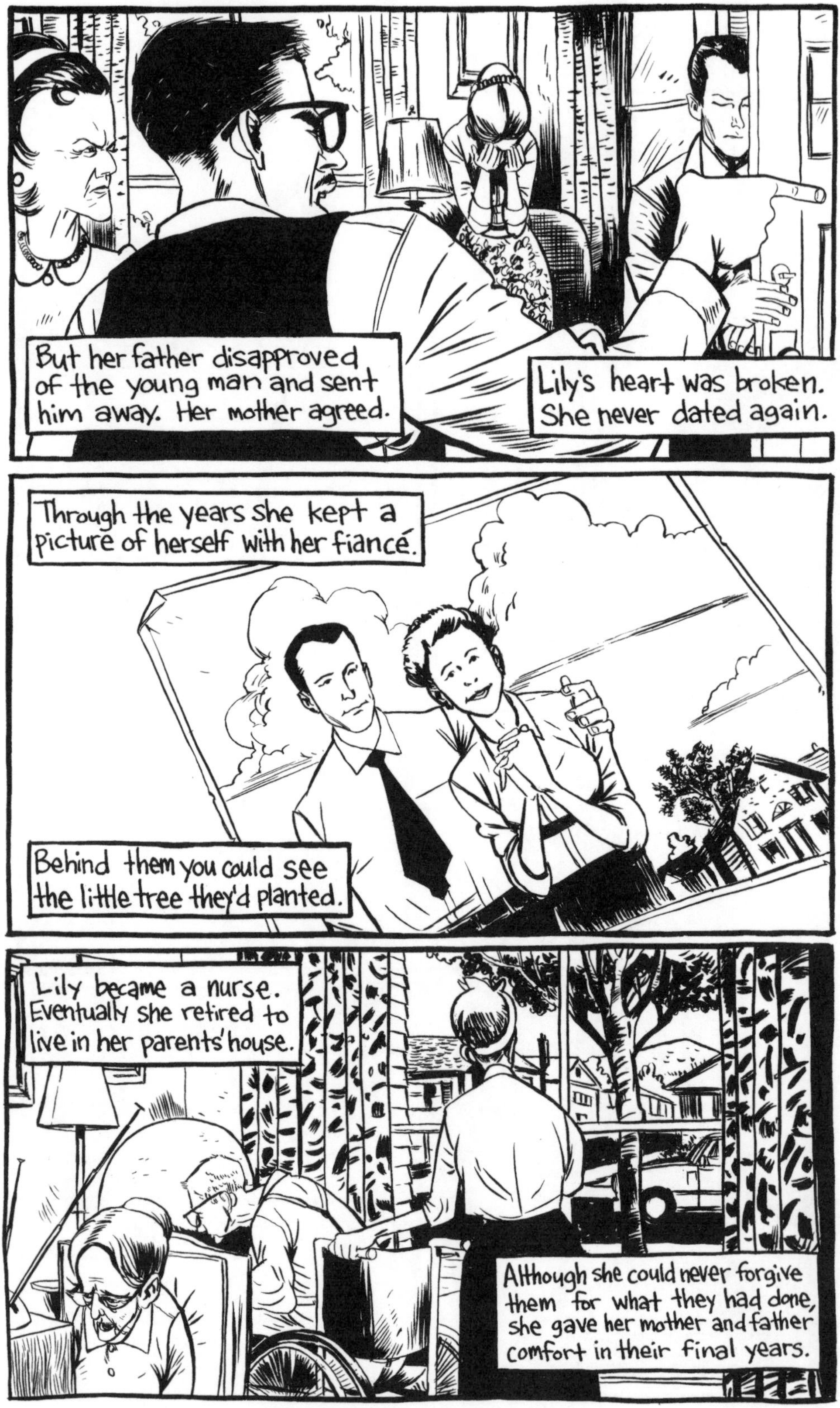

But her father disapproved of the young man and sent him away. Her mother agreed.
Lily's heart was broken. She never dated again.
Through the years she kept a picture of herself with her fiancé.
Behind them you could see the little tree they'd planted.
Lily became a nurse. Eventually she retired to live in her parents' house.
Although she could never forgive them for what they had done, she gave her mother and father comfort in their final years.

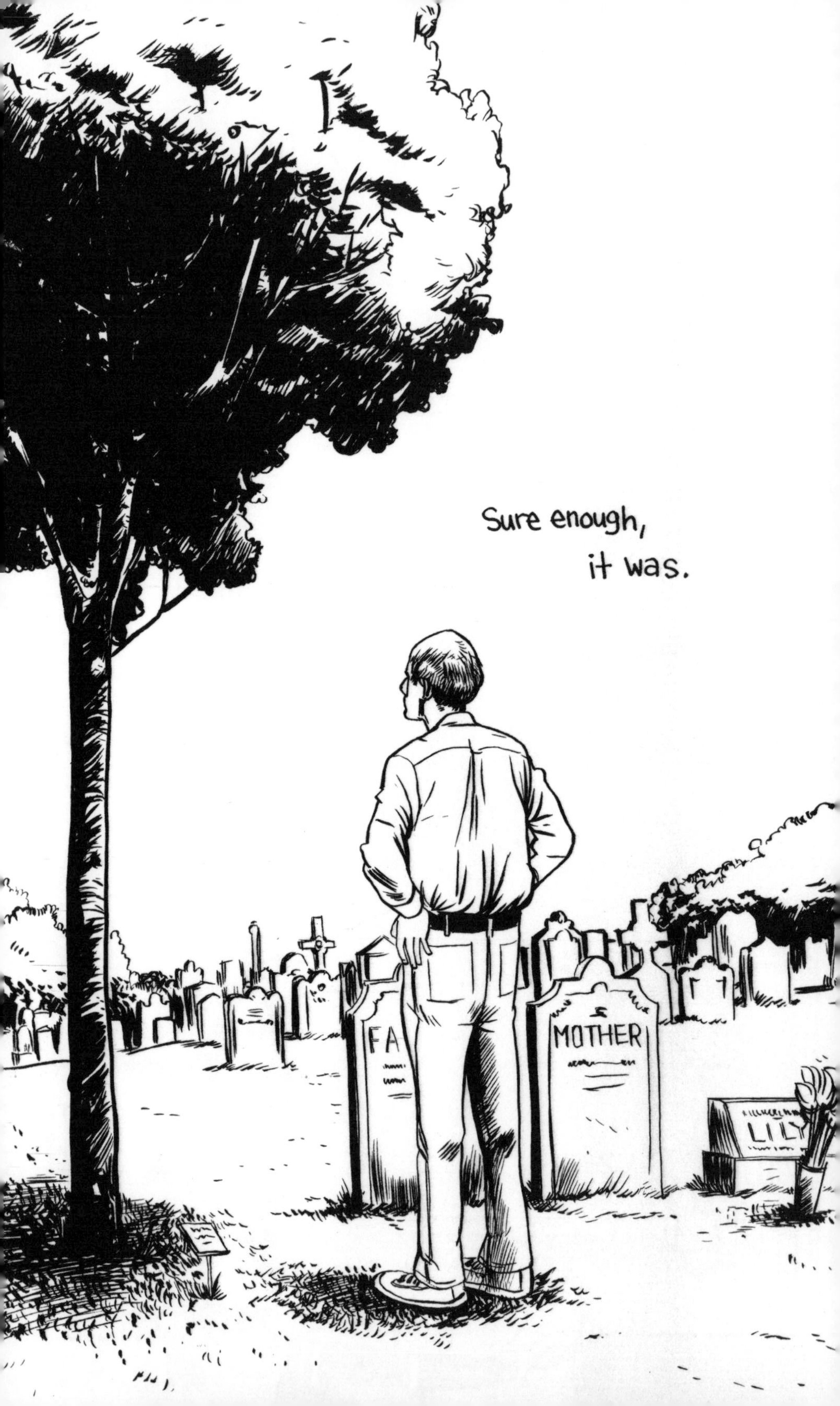
Sure enough,
it was.
FA
MOTHER
LILY

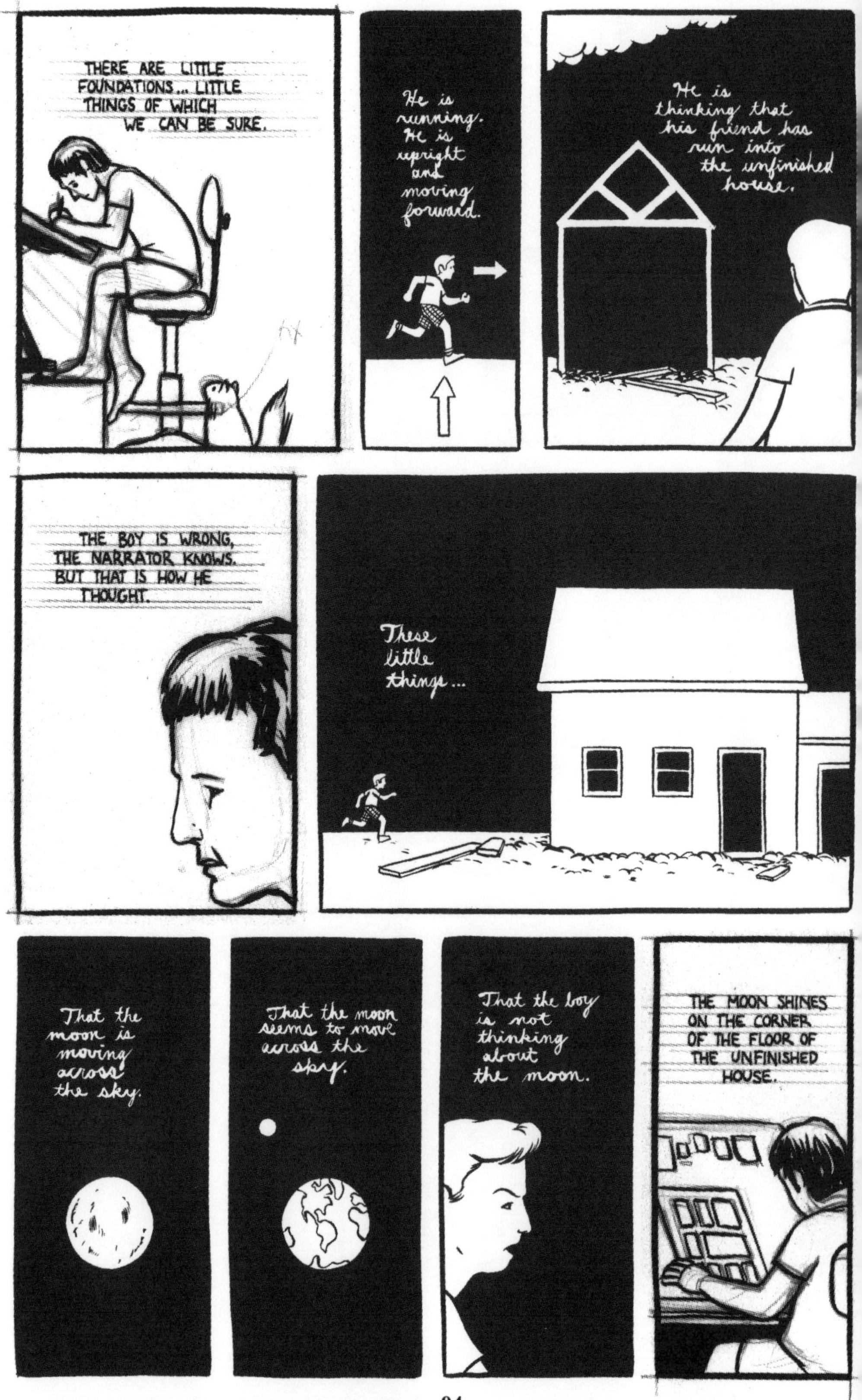
THERE ARE LITTLE FOUNDATIONS... LITTLE THINGS OF WHICH WE CAN BE SURE.
He is running. He is upright and moving forward.
He is thinking that his friend has run into the unfinished house.
THE BOY IS WRONG, THE NARRATOR KNOWS. BUT THAT IS HOW HE THOUGHT.
These little things...
That the moon is moving across the sky.
That the moon seems to move across the sky.
That the boy is not thinking about the moon.
THE MOON SHINES ON THE CORNER OF THE FLOOR OF THE UNFINISHED HOUSE.

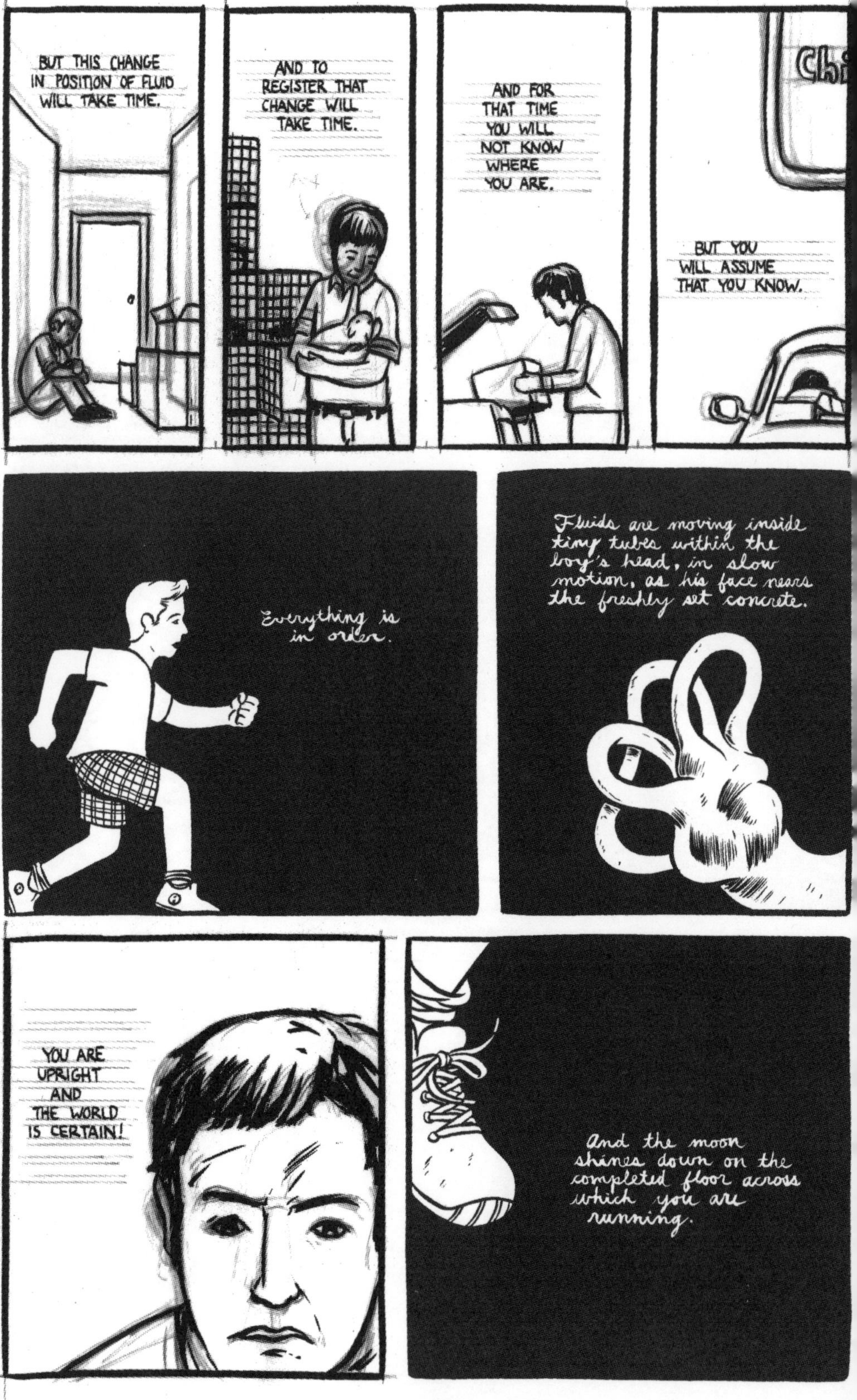
BUT THIS CHANGE IN POSITION OF FLUID WILL TAKE TIME.
AND TO REGISTER THAT CHANGE WILL TAKE TIME.
AND FOR THAT TIME YOU WILL NOT KNOW WHERE YOU ARE.
BUT YOU WILL ASSUME THAT YOU KNOW.
Everything is in order.
Fluids are moving inside tiny tubes within the boy's head, in slow motion, as his face nears the freshly set concrete.
YOU ARE UPRIGHT AND THE WORLD IS CERTAIN!
And the moon shines down on the completed floor across which you are running.

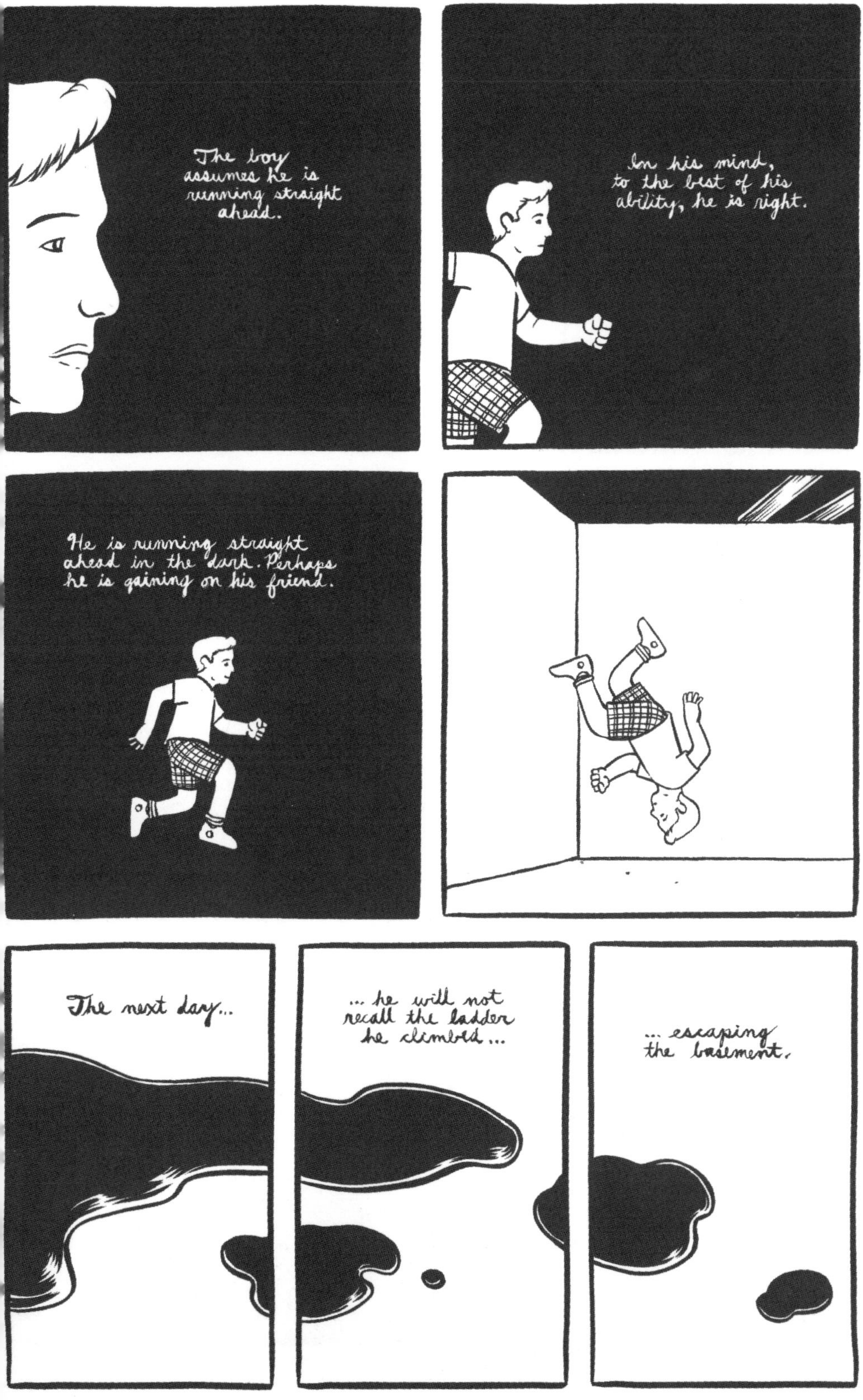
The boy assumes he is running straight ahead.
In his mind, to the best of his ability, he is right.
He is running straight ahead in the dark. Perhaps he is gaining on his friend.
The next day...
... he will not recall the ladder he climbed...
... escaping the basement.

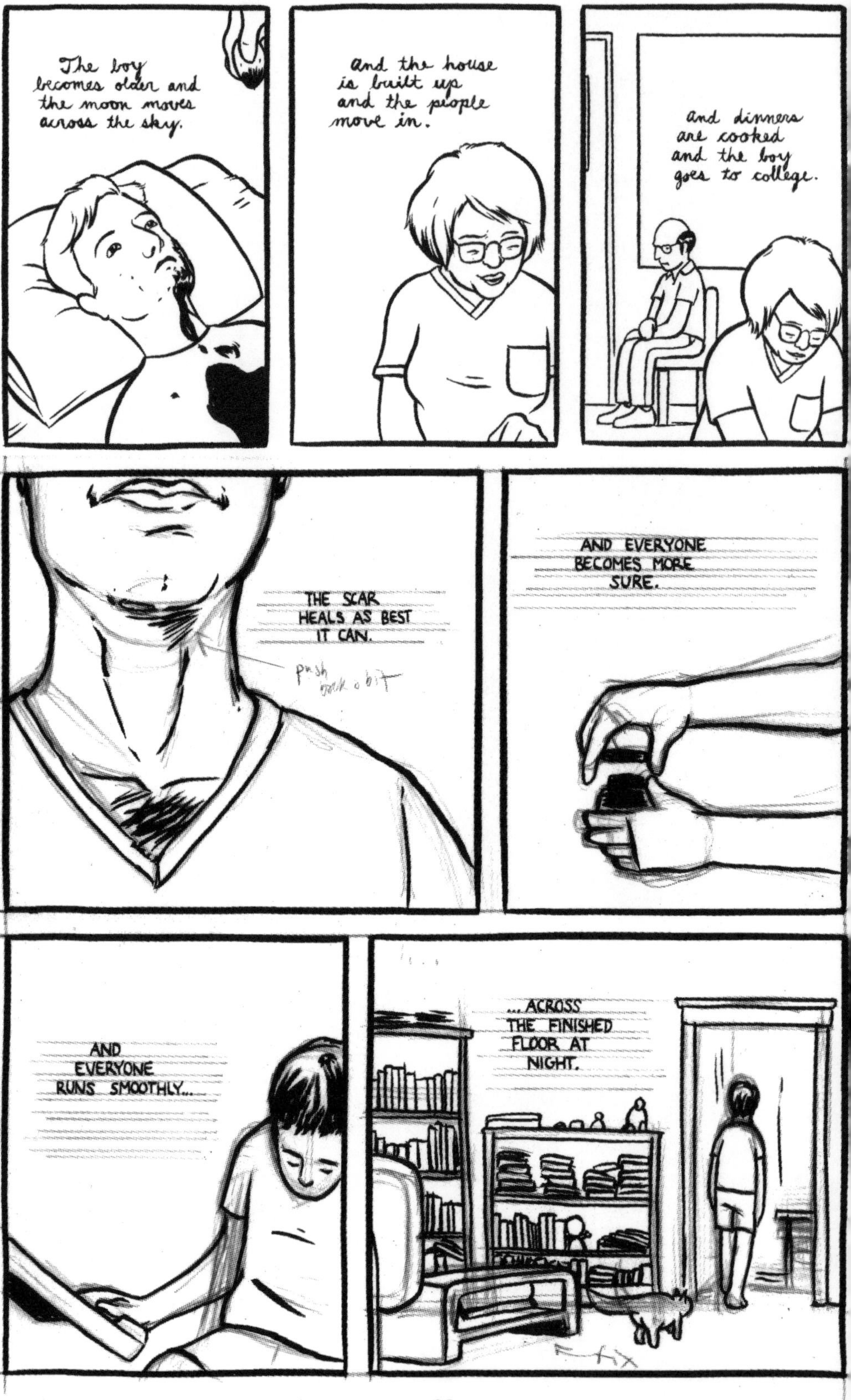
The boy becomes older and the moon moves across the sky.
and the house is built up and the people move in.
and dinners are cooked and the boy goes to college.
THE SCAR HEALS AS BEST IT CAN.
AND EVERYONE BECOMES MORE SURE.
AND EVERYONE RUNS SMOOTHLY...
...ACROSS THE FINISHED FLOOR AT NIGHT.

AFTERWORD

It was Will Eisner, the grand master of sequential art, who noted that comics came of age with the advent of the undergrounds and their cartoonists' insistence on telling stories from real life. It was at that point, says Will, that the medium made the quantum jump beyond its origins as pulp entertainment and into the heady realm of literature. Not surprisingly, Will himself was a pioneer of first-person narrative in comics, albeit in a fictional context; but it remained to those comix artists of the sixties to lend an autobiographical voice to the medium, for the first time establishing close contact between creator and reader.

There is something about the personal voice that is immediately compelling, and not so much because truth often *is* stranger than fiction. Truth, after all, is highly selective at the pen of the writer. Rather, it's the confidences shared and the intimacy of connection that invite the reader's involvement. It's an intimacy, a personal touch, even more pronounced in the case of black-and-white comics, wherein the reader directly feels the physicality of the artist's hand across the page. Inking, as Frank Miller has said on more than one occasion — and evidenced at every turn in *Sin City* — is very sexy!

The cartoonists in this volume are storytellers, by definition. For many, however, this was their first, and courageous, leap into telling real-life stories. And the stories run the gamut: from humorous anecdotes to poignant recollections to philosophical ruminations on life. My thanks go to each of the cartoonists herein, especially to those whom I alternately cajoled or browbeat for their participation, for it is no easy matter to bare one's soul in print.

Thanks are also due to Paul Hornschemeier for his elegant design work and to Katie Moody for her invaluable last-minute editorial assistance — not to mention Mike Richardson for continuing to allow me to work on more personal, less strictly commercial projects.

In the time it took for *AutobioGraphix* to go from production to print, reality intruded in my own life. Eric Lindquist, my boyfriend of fourteen months and a day, died suddenly in his home on July 10, 2003, at the too-young age of 45. I was the one to find him, and that tragic real-life story will haunt me forever. I had talked several times with him about this project, and he took great delight in my excitement as the anthology began to take shape. I regret that Eric did not live long enough to see its completion, and it is to his memory that I would like to dedicate this book.

DIANA SCHUTZ
Portland, Oregon

SERGIO ARAGONÉS
Well known for his humorous marginal strips in *Mad* magazine, multiple
Eisner and Harvey Award winning creator Sergio Aragonés has enjoyed
40 years of success in the world of comics. His popular creator-owned
comic, *Groo*, has now been in print for almost two decades, and the
artist continues to lampoon every subject under the sun in such titles
as *Boogeyman, Louder Than Words*, and *Actions Speak.*

EDDIE CAMPBELL
Eddie Campbell, multi-award winning artist of the groundbreaking
From Hell, is the writer and artist of nine volumes of *Bacchus*, plus
his *Alec* series, which includes *How to Be an Artist, After the Snooter,
The King Canute Crowd*, and *Three Piece Suit.* Additional projects
include Alan Moore's *Snakes & Ladders* and *The Birth Caul*, as well
as *Hellblazer, Uncanny X-Men*, and *Will Eisner's The Spirit:
The New Adventures.* He is currently painting a *Batman* one-shot
for DC Comics that he co-wrote with Daren White.

PAUL CHADWICK
Paul Chadwick grew up in Washington State and earned a B.F.A. in
illustration at Art Center College of Design in 1979. He worked in the
movie business, storyboarding and doing advertising, before pencilling
Dazzler for Marvel in 1984-'85. The next year he premiered *Concrete* in
the first issue of *Dark Horse Presents.* Numerous *Concrete* stories
have appeared there since, as well as in Concrete's own comics
and books. Other works include *The World Below, Gifts of the Night*,
and the upcoming (with Harlan Ellison) *Seven Against Chaos.*

FAREL DALRYMPLE
Xeric Grant winning cartoonist Farel Dalrymple self-published his
staggeringly beautiful book *pop gun war* — a surreal tale of hope and
redemption set against an urban landscape — until it was picked up
by Absence of Ink Press and then collected in graphic novel form by
Dark Horse. A Russ Manning Award nominee, Dalrymple won a 2002
Gold Medal from the Society of Illustrators. His most recent work is
Caper, a miniseries for DC, and he may currently be found in Brooklyn,
at <farel@meathaus.com> and at <www.popgunwar.com>.

RICHARD DOUTT

Richard Doutt has been a landscaper, carpenter, mechanic, and recluse, among other things. He has been married and has been homeless. These days, Doutt is a grandfather and an art student. "The Tree" was written for a class on comics, taught by Diana Schutz. He is honored to be associated with Farel Dalrymple on this project and to be included here with some of the finest cartoonists in the world.

WILL EISNER

Will Eisner is universally acknowledged as one of the great masters of comic book art. Best known for his newspaper comics feature, *The Spirit*, which was syndicated worldwide for a dozen years, Eisner has enjoyed a long and winding career in narrative art. After a stint producing *P.S. Magazine* for the U.S. Army, Eisner returned to comics and since has produced numerous graphic novels, such as *A Contract With God* and, most recently, *Fagin the Jew*. In his mid-eighties, Will Eisner is still at the drawing board every day.

PAUL HORNSCHEMEIER

The Ignatz, Eisner, and Harvey Award nominated creator of *Forlorn Funnies*, Paul Hornschemeier began working on comics while in college, self-publishing his experimental comics series, *Sequential*. His most recent book is the poignant collection of the *Forlorn Funnies* story arc, *Mother, Come Home*. Hornschemeier presently lives in Chicago.

DAN JACKSON

Dan Jackson is the poster boy for multitasking. He digitally colors, inks, corrects, repairs, and occasionally letters comics on a daily and free-lance basis for Dark Horse Comics. He also has the most amazing wife of anyone he knows and the cutest little girl in all the known world.

SEAN KONOT

Letterer Sean Konot has worked with a variety of publishers, including DC, Dark Horse, Maximum Press, Oni Press, and Image. Among his credits are such fan favorites as *Hellboy, Star Wars Tales, Green Arrow, Green Lantern, Harley Quinn,* and *Clerks*. Konot has also lettered stories featuring the characters Batman, Grendel, Catwoman, and Ghost. He currently resides in Seattle.

JASON LUTES

After graduating from the Rhode Island School of Design in 1991, Jason Lutes moved to Seattle, where he drew a serialized comic called "Jar of Fools" for *The Stranger*, a weekly paper. The collected edition of this story is now in its fourth printing through Drawn & Quarterly, which also publishes installments of his ongoing comics novel *Berlin*, a portrait of the German city between the wars. "Rules to Live By" was created during the year he spent in Asheville, NC, before moving back to Seattle in the interest of a lifelong commitment to another person.

LINDA MEDLEY

Linda Medley has garnered critical acclaim and won numerous honors, including several Eisner Awards and a grant from the Xeric Foundation, for her creator-owned series *Castle Waiting*. Medley received a BFA from the Academy of Art in San Francisco, and has illustrated books for Putnam Publishing, Grossett & Dunlap, Houghton Mifflin, and Golden Books, along with work for DC, Dark Horse, Fantagraphics, Image, and Tundra. She currently lives in Portland, Oregon.

METAPHROG

Metaphrog, the Franco-Scottish duo, has been releasing comics since 1996, first serializing *Strange Weather Lately* and *The Maze*. Their current works, including *Louis: Red Letter Day*, *Louis: Lying to Clive*, and *Louis: The Clown's Last Words*, have received multiple Eisner and Ignatz Award nominations and critical acclaim worldwide.

FRANK MILLER

Frank Miller began his career in comics in the '70s, revitalizing Marvel's *Daredevil*. He then took his talents to DC Comics, where he reinvented Batman in 1986 with *Batman: The Dark Knight Returns*. Its recent sequel, the wildly successful *Batman: The Dark Knight Strikes Again*, broke all industry sales records. Prior to this, Miller developed a host of creator-owned projects: *The Big Guy and Rusty the Boy Robot* with Geof Darrow, *Martha Washington* with Dave Gibbons, *Bad Boy* with Simon Bisley, and the multiple award winning *300* with Lynn Varley. The popular *Sin City* series, which Miller both writes and draws, has garnered many Eisner and Harvey Awards while reinvigorating the genre of crime drama.

FÁBIO MOON & GABRIEL BÁ

This duo started drawing comics in 1994, successfully failed at the superhero genre, and so moved on to do their own stories. They have now published two books in Brazil, have short stories in three other anthologies, and have been part of an art show in Spain about new Brazilian comics. Identical twins, Moon and Bá have won awards in Brazil for their independent publications, and received the Xeric Foundation Grant in 1999 to publish the miniseries *Roland: Days of Wrath*, written and self-published by Shane Amaya in the U.S.

BILL MORRISON

From car manual technical studies to advertising to painting some of Disney's most popular animated movie posters, Eisner Award winning Bill Morrison has been a professional illustrator since 1981. He was recruited to draw *The Simpsons* in 1990, and has served as editor, a principal writer, and artist at Bongo Comics since 1994. Fulfilling a lifelong dream, Morrison contributed to Dark Horse's line of Tex Avery titles. Currently Creative Director for Bongo, he is also an art director for Fox's hit animated TV series, *Futurama*.

ARNOLD PANDER

Arnold Pander has been exploring the limits of multimedia, film, and comics with his brother, Jacob, since the Portland, Oregon underground music era of the '80s. They gained national attention in 1986 with Comico's *Grendel*, which led to such works as *Ginger Fox* and the internationally banned *Exquisite Corpse*. In 1990 they co-founded The Fuse Gallery, a collective of Portland art and performance spaces, and, in 1998, the production company Radius Pictures. Along with Arnold's 1997 *Secret Broadcast*, a CD inspired by pirate radio, the brothers have teamed up to depict futuristic cityscapes in Vertigo's *Accelerate* and the ambitious *Triple•X* for Dark Horse.

STAN SAKAI

Stan Sakai was born in Kyoto, Japan, grew up in Hawaii, and now lives in California with his wife, Sharon, and two children, Hannah and Matthew. His creation, *Usagi Yojimbo*, first appeared in comics in 1984. Since then, Usagi has been on television as a guest of the *Teenage Mutant Ninja Turtles* and has been made into toys, seen on clothing, and featured in a series of trade paperback collections. Sakai is also an award-winning letterer for his work on the *Spider-Man* Sunday newspaper strips, *Usagi Yojimbo*, and Sergio Aragonés' *Groo the Wanderer*. Sakai is a recipient of a Parents' Choice Award, an Inkpot Award, multiple Eisner Awards, an American Library Association Award, a National Cartoonists Society Comic Book Division Award, and two Spanish Haxtur Awards.

DIANA SCHUTZ

Diana Schutz is a senior editor at Dark Horse Comics and an adjunct instructor of comics history and criticism at Portland Comunity College.

WILLIAM STOUT

William Stout has worked as a designer on over 30 feature films. He has also been the key creator for a variety of Disney, Lucasfilm/Industrial Light and Magic, MCA/Universal, and DreamWorks SKG projects. Stout is perhaps best known for his depictions of dinosaurs that have been published and exhibited in museums worldwide, inspiring both *The Land Before Time* and *Jurassic Park*. His illustration work has won a host of honors, including two Gold Awards and one Silver Award from the Society of Illustrators. His current projects include writing and illustrating the first visual history of life in Antarctica.

MATT WAGNER

Matt Wagner is best known for his highly respected creator-owned titles, *Grendel* and *Mage*, but he has also worked on *Sandman Mystery Theatre*, two successive *Batman/Grendel* crossovers as well as various other *Batman* titles, and a run of covers for the *Lone Wolf and Cub* series. In 1998 Wagner returned to the Hunter Rose incarnation of Grendel, in the multiple Eisner Award-winning miniseries — *Grendel: Black, White, & Red* — and followed with *Grendel: Red, White, & Black*, while also painting covers for DC's *Green Arrow* series. His latest project is DC's best-selling and critically acclaimed *Trinity*.

More graphic novels from Dark Horse Books

Sergio Aragonés
Actions Speak
ISBN 1-56971-758-3
Boogeyman
ISBN 1-56971-374-X
Louder Than Words
ISBN 1-56971-343-X
The Groo Collection
various ISBNs

Paul Chadwick's *Concrete*
Fragile Creature
ISBN 1-56971-022-8
Killer Smile
ISBN 1-56971-080-5
Strange Armor
ISBN 1-56971-335-9
Think Like a Mountain
ISBN 1-56971-176-3
The Complete Concrete
ISBN 1-56971-037-6

Farel Dalrymple
pop gun war
ISBN 1-56971-934-9

Will Eisner
Last Day in Vietnam
ISBN 1-56971-500-9
The Will Eisner Sketchbook
ISBN 1-56971-960-8

Paul Hornschemeier
Mother, Come Home
ISBN 1-59307-037-3

Linda Medley
Castle Waiting: The Curse of Brambly Hedge
ISBN 1-59307-081-0

Frank Miller's *Sin City*
The Art of Sin City
ISBN 1-56971-818-0
Sin City
ISBN 1-878574-59-0
A Dame to Kill For
ISBN 1-56971-068-6
The Big Fat Kill
ISBN 1-56971-171-2
That Yellow Bastard
ISBN 1-56971-225-5
Family Values
ISBN 1-56971-313-8
Hell and Back
ISBN 1-56971-481-9
Booze, Broads, & Bullets
ISBN 1-56971-366-9

Arnold & Jacob Pander
Triple•X
ISBN 1-56971-218-2

Stan Sakai's *Usagi Yojimbo*
The Brink of Life and Death
ISBN 1-56971-297-2
Demon Mask
ISBN 1-56971-523-8
Duel at Kitanoji
ISBN 1-56971-973-X
Grasscutter
ISBN 1-56971-413-4
Grasscutter II
ISBN 1-56971-660-9
Grey Shadows
ISBN 1-56971-459-2
Seasons
ISBN 1-56971-375-8
Shades of Death
ISBN 1-56971-259-X
The Shrouded Moon
ISBN 1-56971-883-0
Space Usagi
ISBN 1-56971-290-5

Matt Wagner's *Grendel*
Black, White, & Red
ISBN 1-56971-493-2
The Devil Inside
ISBN 1-56971-604-8
Devil's Legacy
ISBN 1-56971-662-5
Devil Tales
ISBN 1-56971-428-2
War Child
ISBN 1-878574-89-2

Various
Dark Horse Maverick: Happy Endings
ISBN 1-56971-820-2